Good Mourning

MOVING THROUGH
EVERYDAY LOSSES
WITH WISDOM FROM
THE OTHER SIDE

THERESA CAPUTO

WITH KRISTINA GRISH

HarperOne
An Imprint of HarperCollinsPublishers

HarperOne

HarperCollins books may be purchased for educational, business, or sales promotional use. For information, please email the Special Markets Department at SPsales@harpercollins.com.

FIRST EDITION

Designed by Nancy Singer

Library of Congress Cataloging-in-Publication Data is available upon request.

ISBN 978-0-06-301456-5

20 21 22 23 24   LSC   10 9 8 7 6 5 4 3 2 1

I've experienced more than my share of daily losses these past few years, and I'd like to dedicate this book to my original support system from Day 1: my parents, Ronnie and Nick; my kids, Larry and Victoria; my brother, Michael; and my cousin Lisa. I'm also grateful to the team that helps me bring healing to others every day, including Courtney Mullin, Victoria Woods, Jeff Cohen, Magilla Entertainment, TLC, Rich Super, and Mills Entertainment. Finally, I dedicate this book to my clients, who allow me to share my gift with them.

And to God and Spirit, without whom I would not be where I am today.

CONTENTS

WHAT ARE YOUR EVERYDAY LOSSES?

I've been communicating with souls on the other side almost my whole life—since I was four years old, actually. It wasn't until I was in my late twenties, however, that I began to communicate with my own deceased loved ones and the loved ones of others while taking a spiritual awareness class. After learning firsthand how hard it is for people on this plane to heal after a death, I decided to use my gifts to help others move through the grief they feel when a loved one passes. Working as a medium for the past twenty years or so, I now talk to these heavenly souls— the angels, guides, and departed loved ones whom I refer to as Spirit—for a living. And all day, every day, they deliver messages that bring about the highest good for all concerned. These spiritual beings love, guide, and protect us from the other side, and they have taught me everything I know not just about life after death, but about the beautiful yet challenging life we're all engaging in right now.

What's fascinating is that these voices from the other side

tell me that death is not the only type of loss that burdens our souls. Navigating our time on this earthly plane includes not just coping with a loved one's passing, but more often, and sometimes more profoundly, making sense of the losses that we face every day, which tend to be undervalued and underacknowledged but have the potential to plummet us into shock, depression, anxiety, and other forms of grief. These daily losses include losing a house; a spouse to divorce; our health, hopes, and dreams; our youth, trust, control; our identity, financial stability, independence; our faith; our will to endure; our security, and more.

DAILY LOSSES 101

Every one of us experiences daily losses, and often more than one, on a regular basis. These losses can be big or small. We can see them coming or they can completely blindside us. They can tear us down or make us stronger. Everyday losses are unfortunately part of life on this planet, as we go about making both free-will and destined choices that affect us and other people. Daily losses are a hurdle that we must anticipate and then jump over, always expecting that others are around the corner.

Spirit wants you to be prepared for these losses, because the more you learn about how to cope with them, the less jarring it will be the next time you encounter them. I'm not saying it will get easier to deal with the grief that comes from these losses, but it will be less of a shock to the system. You will recognize a daily loss, know what to do, and recover much faster.

Knowing how to identify and heal from daily losses is essential because they can cause serious emotional damage if we don't address and process them; their effects can build on each other and make us feel worse as time goes on. All of us experience daily losses—every person who picks up this book can relate. And while some of us feel grief more severely than others, we all experience it in a way that is specific to our personality and what's happened in our past. Only one thing is universal: there's no way around such grief; we have to move through it.

We do have control over the way we handle our everyday losses, though. As we mourn what once was, it can be a life-changing ordeal in either a positive or a negative way. My hope is that when you're hit with an everyday loss, this book, with Spirit's help, will steer you toward positive solutions for mourning and help you change your life for the better. In the next chapter, Spirit and I address the topic of daily losses more specifically so that you can appreciate what they are and how they impact the body, mind, and soul. For now, it's enough to know that these are emotional roadblocks and getting over them can lead to lessons learned.

SPIRIT: THE ULTIMATE EDITOR

When I write a book, I follow Spirit's editorial direction to a T— and boy, do they deliver. I first got a nudge from my guides to cover the topic of everyday losses when I began to notice during readings that clients had a harder time recovering from the loss of a loved one if they hadn't dealt with other losses, that is, everyday losses, first. And then Spirit showed me that these losses could often feel as emotionally traumatizing as losing a loved one, and they felt this subject warranted a book devoted to how to navigate these issues. Well—*voilà*. This is that divinely guided book.

As you move through these pages, there are a few things Spirit would like you to keep in mind. First, the topics covered in each chapter are those that come up most commonly during readings related to grief. Spirit dictated the order of the chapters too, which follow an intuitive flow though you are more than welcome to skip around, depending on how the subjects resonate with you. Spirit also guided me and my collaborator to the stories, some of which are full of strange coincidences. You'll notice that a few of the names repeat, and sometimes the chapters have themes. For instance, in Chapter 9 about losing a home, Spirit included two stories about fires—one with an accidental cause and one caused by a natural disaster. And Chapter 19 about losing a body part focuses strongly on women's health and related illnesses. When this kind of thing happens, I've learned that Spirit is drawing our attention to a warning or theme—and in these cases, I suspect that these stories contain important matters that will speak to you. Ending each chapter is an exercise—a "Good Mourning"—that Spirit felt would help you with the mourning process specific to that chapter's topic, as well as an affirmation that I channeled from Spirit.

So as you set out to face and move through your daily losses, let this book be your guide. Earmark your favorite pages, journal about what you learn, and get crafty with the exercises. Underline passages and then pass the book on to a friend once you've finished it. I want you to use this book and digest its words in your soul. I want it to move you to recognize, then feel, then act, and then heal. Together, we will get you to a place of peace and understanding. Spirit and I hope that you will find this book as helpful to use as it was fascinating to channel and write. Enjoy.

While I'm writing this, our world is in the midst of a global health crisis as we battle the novel Coronavirus pandemic. Keeping ourselves, our families, and our communities safe and healthy has meant going about our everyday routines in brand-new ways, from how we shop to how (or whether) we socialize. While I feel that all precautions have been necessary, they have inadvertently led to a number of unforeseen, daily losses for the average person. For me and most of my friends and family, plus clients and those I read or hear about in the news, our mutual heartbreaks have included *nearly every topic* that we discuss in this freaking book! While the pandemic has been a tremendous burden on our minds, bodies, and spirits (to say the least . . .), Spirit says that we all must stay strong. What's more, we need to respect, love, and honor each other—while releasing fear and embracing faith—until we get to the other side of this problem.

Though I certainly didn't know it when I wrote *Good Mourning* before the pandemic occurred (in fact, God and Spirit nudged me to write about the daily loss topic back in 2018!), this book couldn't be more timely for those of us who struggle to overcome unexpected grief, calm anxieties, and find peace and happiness in our crazy world right now.

1

A LOSS IS A LOSS

We immediately associate grief with the loss of a loved one, but you can grieve the loss of anything you once loved and cherished. With any loss, you grieve what once was.

Of course, grief is much more straightforward when we lose someone. We are immediately thrown into it and know how to recognize it and what to call it. We recognize the death as a loss, participate in rituals that honor the deceased, and seek out established support to help us move through this painful experience. When it comes to daily losses, however, we usually think of them as bad luck or an upsetting turn of events—rarely worthy of a mourning process. But the thing is, daily losses can cause real emotional damage, and Spirit says a lot of the reason for this is precisely *because* we don't understand why an event other than a death—like a divorce or losing a job or home—could cause such profound pain.

We don't recognize our gutted feelings for what they are, so we don't know how to process them. As a result, we might think we're in a vague depression or suddenly prone to panic attacks, but what we're experiencing is grief, deep and profound. Our grief will then cause confusing, negative emotions to snowball, and what might begin as depression or panic will evolve into a complicated soup of anger, guilt, self-reproach, loneliness, shock, disbelief, confusion, social withdrawal, restlessness, obsessive thinking, sleep and appetite issues . . . stop me anytime. Before we know it, we're imprisoned by our emotions.

Spirit says one of the reasons that daily losses can be so traumatic is because most of them involve multiple unprocessed feelings at once. For example, grieving the loss of function after an accident or the diagnosis of a chronic illness could lead to grieving the loss of a prior life, future dreams, control, support, comfort, familiarity, stable finances, and faith in God. Because daily losses eat away at our souls in such a huge and unappreciated way, Spirit says it's time to pay attention to the most common daily losses and figure out how to recover from them.

HOW DOES THIS MAKE YOU FEEL?

When I channel for clients experiencing grief from daily loss, I find that the experience supports what psychologists in the physical world also say about grief—that losses come with ramifications that are physical (headaches, insomnia, lack of appetite), emotional (sadness, depression, guilt), cognitive (obsessive thinking, inability to concentrate), behavioral (crying, avoiding others), and spiritual (searching for meaning or losing faith in God). Yet once you name these feelings, recognize the losses, and create mourning rituals around them, you can move through the pain and begin to heal. It isn't just a good idea to grieve these types of troubling events— bottom line, it's *essential,* so you can then settle into a new normal or fresh beginning for yourself. If you don't process these losses, you will start to see yourself in a negative way that's colored with unresolved grief and unprocessed feelings. This takes a toll on your self-esteem and how you view your place in the world.

Because Spirit says that all grief is our natural reaction to loss, and is caused by the end of, or change in, what once was, a daily loss isn't that different from a death. *A loss is a loss.* Whether you're missing a person who died or your Nana's treasured bracelet, you don't have someone or something in your life anymore and you miss it—you grieve it. You want it back. And as with a death, everyone grieves in their own way and at their own pace. It's said that we feel our own losses at 100 percent, no matter what they are—and no loss is more important than the other. I agree. You have every right to feel the way you do.

Spirit also says that you can't compare your losses and grief to those of another person, because every one of us responds to loss and grief differently. Just as you can't compare the way a parent feels after a child's death to that of a wife who loses her husband, you can't compare how upset a person might feel after losing their home in a natural disaster to what it's like to lose a sense of safety after experiencing a trauma. Comparison-based thoughts diminish everyone's experiences and aren't helpful in the grief process. Comparing your loss with that of others won't help you feel better and it doesn't prove that your loss is somehow worse than someone else's. Besides, this isn't the time to one-up a fellow griever.

What might be more beneficial to understanding and validating your feelings is knowing that the more you identify with a situation you're grieving, the more intense your grief. This adds some logic to balance out your emotions. So how connected are your emotions and identity to the necklace you lost? To the partner you're divorcing? To the career you left behind? To the investments that went bust? This helps determine how deeply your grief hurts and resonates.

Spirit suggests you try to find some comfort in the fact that we all experience daily losses on a regular basis; we are in good company. Maybe if we thought about grief as a normal way of existing in this world, rather than as a series of tragic one-off events in our lives, we'd feel better prepared to grieve daily losses as they come up. If you think about it, you lose things that you love all the time—arguments, free time, a garden's flowers or trees when the seasons change. Life is all about transition. It takes both joy and pain to grow our souls, and this process insists that we always put one foot in front of the other and carry on.

STEPPING INTO GRIEF

The grief process for daily losses is similar to that of death. You will experience the typical five steps of denial, anger, bargaining, depression, and acceptance in an order that is right for you. You might skip some of these steps or linger on a few of them longer than others. And your grief process may take years to move through. You will grieve an absence and perhaps always hold a degree of sadness in your heart and soul for what's missing, while learning to let the rest go. In both cases, you must accept the loss and learn to move on from it in a way that's right for you.

The most important factor in moving through grief in a healthy way is having hope and support and creating mourning rituals around your daily loss. Spirit suggests you join a nonjudgmental support group, find a therapist, share your feelings with a small army of thoughtful friends, and try to find a new normal among people who've experienced similar losses or can help you understand yours. Explore ways to mourn and express your feelings such as keeping a journal to record your feelings, choices, and decisions; or joining or engaging in activities that let you get your grief out, even if you do them on your own. Taking long walks or making yourself a cup of tea every afternoon can encourage you to slow down. Learning to say no, treating yourself to a new haircut, getting a facial, taking a long bath, getting a massage, and generally putting your oxygen mask on first will help you get through the backlash of a daily loss. Creating alters or angel corners in your home with photos, crystals, figurines, and other things that make you happy will lift you from the burden of daily losses too. An essential oils atomizer and meditation app can also lift your spirits and please your senses when you're in the thick of grief.

Daily losses put wear and tear on our physical, emotional, and spiritual bodies, so it's super important to be sure you're kind to yourself as you grieve these insults. Your ultimate goal is to function and thrive again in the world, set and achieve new goals, feel happiness again, and be able to soon say that you have both survived the worst and are thriving in your new reality. Until then, it is simply enough to get a little stronger, and a little better, every day.

No matter what avenues you take, grieving your daily losses will help to keep your feelings and soul lighter and brighter, which allows you to live your best life. It's also important because when a loved one does die, you want your soul to be as free of burdens as possible in order to grieve that loss. A lot of times, the souls of departed loved ones say that you have to grieve certain other losses before you can grieve their death. If you lost your job and then your dad died, and you never dealt with that first loss, then the grief from your father's passing will be significantly harder to manage. Spirit wants you to prevent the emotional pile-on that makes it harder to heal.

WHEN HEAVEN WINKS

When clients are grieving a daily loss, I find that they are buoyed by support that Spirit offers them through cool signs, awe-inspiring dreams, their own belief systems, faith, and the like. Our angels, the souls of departed loved ones, and our spirit guides place helpful and comforting signs, people, and opportunities in our path to help us make better choices and decisions. These interventions help us grow, live, and learn if we choose to accept and embrace them. What's tricky is that if you are too caught up in your grief, you might not be receptive to the signs and the guidance that God and the universe send your way. You might miss them or feel somehow turned off by them. It's also very easy to become so consumed with your sorrow that Spirit can't penetrate your energy to bring your awareness to a sign or break through it to appear in a dream.

Mantra: I may be facing a loss, but I'm gaining wisdom and growing every day.

The good news is that because Spirit's intention is to always tell you that you're being loved, protected, and guided from the other side, Spirit will do what they can to get your attention and give you the reassurance you crave. I tend to smell cigarette smoke as a sign, which is my paternal grandmother Nanny Brigandi's soul saying hello, and when I find a random dime on the floor or in my bag, I know the soul of my departed Gram, my maternal grandmother, is reassuring me that she's with me. What's wild is that if you're oblivious to the birds, butterflies, license plates, and other common signs that Spirit sends, they might simply work through another person to get their point across.

I'll never forget the time when I was grieving the fact that I could no longer attend Sunday dinners with my family because I was too busy with my insane schedule. I'd be running around like crazy while missing my family time. Passing on those meals was a loss of comfort and security for me, and I grieved them. When my frustration reached its peak, my cousin Lisa called to tell me she had seen a big, fat fly, which is a symbol that Nanny Brigandi sends me when I need a little oomph. As soon as I acknowledged that this hairy bug was a sign for me, I instinctively felt that the message was telling me to slow down and breathe, because I was missing out on what mattered.

It's hard to see signs when we're harried. At the end of the day, guidance is always there for us. It's up to us to soften and lean in to the universe's messages, becoming more aware of the signs and symbols around us, so we can embrace them.

Dreams are another sign that Spirit sends us when we need emotional reinforcement as we grieve daily losses. Dreams are intended to let us know that we're going to be okay and to let go of the fears and regrets that stress us out. They encourage us to move forward with faith in knowing that whatever happens is the best thing at that time. After my Gram passed, I grieved the loss of her house. That home held so many special memories for me, and I had a hard time picturing another family enjoying it the way that we had. One night I dreamed of Gram sitting at her kitchen table, crying, and when I asked her why she was so upset, she said she was crying happy tears. "I'm so thrilled that you're coming to have breakfast," her soul told me, "because I have to tell you that it's time to let the house go. And it's okay." Then I woke up. Later that day, I called my mom to tell her about the dream. Do you know what she said? "We sold Gram's house today." Un-freaking-believable! What's crazier is that this was the first time I'd dreamed of a loved one's soul, and the dream validated that it was time for me to let the house go, as well as the grief I felt around its sale.

Finally, from a spiritual perspective, one of the most important reasons that Spirit wants you to properly grieve your daily losses is so that you can learn lessons from them. Every one of us has spiritual lessons to learn that, based on our choices and decisions in the physical world, will grow our souls eternally. Your learned lessons also determine where your soul resides on the other side (known as a "level") after you die and make you feel whole while you're still here on earth. Spirit insists that you're in the physical world to be taught lessons in various ways—your life has a purpose, and things happen for a reason. Therefore, how you react to your daily losses factors into lessons related to compassion, kindness, patience, and other values that God prioritizes.

Now when I mention God, I'm referring to an all-knowing energy that goes by a lot of other names too—the universe, Allah, Source, to name a few—depending on a person's preference or belief system. I refer to this beautiful and powerful entity as God because I'm Roman Catholic, and I use the pronoun "He" to refer to God, but you can call God by any name that's meaningful to you. Know, too, that the faster you learn God's lessons for you, the more you'll understand your own soul and trust your intuition and the guidance that He lays out for you every day.

Ready to understand and work through your daily losses? The grief process is never easy, but with Spirit's help, it'll be just what your soul needs to heal.

Good Mourning

Now that you understand what an everyday loss is, think about the times you've recently suffered and how you've grieved, or pushed away grief, not realizing what that feeling truly was. Next, close your eyes, choose one daily loss that still sticks with you, and sit quietly with the emotions that bubble up when you think about it. What do you feel? Where do you feel the sadness, anger, and/or vulnerability in your body? Visualize a ball of white light entering your body through the top of your head and use it to wash away the negative feelings about this loss. Imagine it pushing out any darkness or bad feelings that you hold in your body that are related to your grief. Do this for five minutes, or until you feel calmer and lighter than when you began.

2

ON LOSING A FRIEND

When a relationship with a friend whom you deeply care about ends, you can feel as if you've been cracked wide open and your world has turned upside down—in other words, not that different from how you feel when a loved one dies. Perhaps the reason you're no longer friends is because you moved away, you had a falling out, you have different interests, you found yourselves at different life stages, or you felt your priorities shift in opposing directions. Do any of those sound familiar? No matter what the cause of your split, this loss is riddled with physical, emotional, and spiritual ramifications.

Losing a friend can be especially painful if you don't even know why the friendship ended. When I first got engaged to my now ex-husband, Larry, my best friend stopped speaking to me, and to this day, I don't know why. I'm not sure whether I said or did something to upset her, but I regret whatever it was that occurred and how I must have made her feel. I remember hearing that her husband had passed, and then I coincidentally ran into her years later. I wanted to help her connect to her husband's soul, but I was still new to my gift and shy about it, so I never offered. I later found out that my friend's father had passed as well, and I could only imagine how devastated she must have felt because first she had lost her husband, and then she no longer had her dad, to whom she always had been so close. When I ran into her that day, she still appeared angry, perhaps at me or at life, it wasn't clear; and I couldn't help but think that if we were in a different place, I could have helped comfort her. Instead, we parted ways again, and I haven't seen her since. Not knowing why she was so upset with me was almost as hard as not having her in my life anymore. It's a shame because we could have shared the ups and downs of raising kids, losing loved ones, and supporting each other the way that friends do.

A friend can be your soul mate—a spiritual twin who values your hopes, dreams, and heartaches as much as you do. You share your deepest secrets and a common language of inside jokes and memories. Good friends are there for you when you need them most, and they simply "get it." It takes a lot to fill the hole their absence leaves behind.

WHEN YOU'RE BLUER THAN A SMURF

So why are friendship breakups so painful? Spirit says it's because a good friend sees you at your worst *and* your best. It's a great friend who throws you a surprise party when you feel forgotten and dog-sits your pug when nobody else can. She's nice to your parents in person and then validates their craziness over a glass of wine once she's alone with you. A friend steps in as your plus-one to a dinner party when your spouse is sick and rushes to your side when he tells you he wants a divorce. She keeps your secrets and can read your mind. Sometimes the best Friday nights involve ordering takeout together while watching reruns of *Hoarding: Buried Alive.*

So when a friendship changes or shifts or dissolves, for whatever reason, and regardless of whether you or the other person initiated the divide, Spirit says you can feel abandoned and perhaps even betrayed. You've lost your sidekick and security blanket, all at once. With romantic relationships, you know there's always a chance that it might not work out, but with a friendship, you let your guard down quickly and expect to be unconditionally accepted no matter what. When things end, you feel like you're losing part of yourself because your identities are so intertwined.

Spirit says that losing a friend affects every corner of your life, and I agree. It puts a dent in your social circle, because you feel funny going places and seeing people that you have in common. Just the thought of bumping into an ex-friend could lead to uncomfortable anxiety or a stress-related condition like irritable bowel syndrome. You could also get depressed and isolate yourself from the friends you still have. Those relationships might then suffer in turn.

Bottom line, when you lose a friend, you lose a significant piece of your heart. Even so, Spirit wants you to remember that you are not alone in your grief. The beauty of everyday loss is that other people experience similar difficulties that come with living on this physical plane. When you're at the mall or in line at the market buying cucumbers for dinner and you're pushing back tears because you're thinking of your friend, know that the people around you might also be grieving in their own ways. They might be missing a spouse deployed overseas in combat or struggling with how to pay their mortgage. Everyone faces daily losses and fights to find peace and love—and pushes away fear—just like you; they also try to hold it together to get through the day.

GO EASY ON YOURSELF

If you're suffering the loss of a friend, Spirit says to take care of yourself during this time. You have to learn to let go of the relationship and live without the person you cared about. Survival is a must. You have no choice but to fight through the pain. Spirit says that if an emotion hurts your soul, then it doesn't serve a positive purpose, and you need to let it go so that you can heal.

When a friendship ends, one of the worst blocks to healing is blaming the other person for its breakdown. Blame is one of the ugliest default actions we can take because our souls grow from honesty and accountability. If you don't practice this while you're on this plane, Spirit says it's one of the top lessons you will have to re-experience through another person's eyes and learn on the other side. Own your role in the friendship's dissolution. Ask yourself what you could have done differently. Spirit says that blame doesn't solve problems, and you simply go around and around in your head on an argument that's one-sided. Instead, try to become aware of the areas where you may have fallen short as a friend; this could help you improve future relationships.

Mantra: I'm thankful for what
I've learned from past friendships,
so I can be a better friend in the future.

When you lose a friend, you have to be careful of emotional triggers. Spirit says you might feel sad when you pass a restaurant you used to go to or flip past a movie on TV that you used to watch together. In so many ways, because you've lost a relationship, it can feel a lot like a romantic breakup. You'll need to find new activities and social events to keep yourself occupied. Spirit says to join activities that introduce you to new friends and do what you can to change your daily routine. I stopped smoking twenty-seven years ago, but I still crave a cigarette and grieve this ritual when I'm in a social environment—especially when I'm drinking a vodka cranberry! You could easily say that I grieve smoking like an old friend. In the same way, you will find yourself in environments or situations that prompt you to want something that's no longer yours or even good for you.

CAN YOU EVER MAKE UP AFTER A BREAKUP?

So are all friendship losses final? Sometimes you do have a chance to reunite, both in the afterlife and here on earth. In the afterlife, you may have an opportunity to make nice with broken friendships. Oftentimes when I channel, a departed friend will come through and apologize for cruel words or a deed that caused hurt. This usually comes about as a means of redemption for the soul, after going through a life review where the soul has to relive certain pinnacle events through another person's eyes. This helps the soul to grow and learn lessons. Here, the souls of friends often say they're sorry for making a person feel disappointed or not hearing their side of a story—and they always take responsibility for their actions.

The most positive way to frame this loss, then, is to learn from it before your soul is forced to learn this lesson after you pass. While you're still here, Spirit suggests journaling about the experience; I find that when I do this, I become aware of my words and behaviors, and areas in which I can improve come floating to the surface of my consciousness. Maybe a lost friendship will encourage you to become a better listener, to be more empathetic to another person's problems, or to make a greater effort with new friends in the future. Maybe you'll get the chance to start over.

The topic of friends who've been lost and then found again reminds me of a woman I know named Nicole who lived with her best friend Ashley and Ashley's family during Nicole's freshman year of college. This arrangement allowed Nicole to save money and enjoy all the comforts of home at her bestie's house. Ashley's parents were pastors at a church, so Nicole initially felt comfortable and safe in her friend's place. She had also known Ashley's family since she was eleven years old and said, "Her family had become my family over the years."

Yet shortly after Nicole moved in, Ashley's father began to sexually abuse Nicole—several times over about six months. He would inappropriately touch Nicole, apologize, and then do it again. "There were a lot of mind games," Nicole told me, "with the dad saying he wished he were younger, that he'd be jealous when I started dating, and that if I told, his family and career would be destroyed. It turned me upside down."

In no time, Nicole felt trapped in her situation; she became depressed and wanted to die. "I remember sitting on a bench in front of a lake for hours, trying to convince myself to jump in with weights so that I'd drown and disappear from the situation," she said. "I loved my friend and her family, and they had been such a blessing to me through the years—I didn't want to be the cause of her family being destroyed." Can you imagine? "That's the power of manipulation," she said. "Someone was destroying me, but I wanted to protect *them* from being destroyed."

It took Nicole six months to tell Ashley about her father's behavior. Ashley immediately believed her and told the rest of her family. Within hours, Nicole was safely moved out of the home but was forced to leave college for financial reasons. "As it was, I had a rough upbringing [her father was addicted to drugs and suicidal, and her single mom prioritized her relationships with others over Nicole and her sister], had just graduated from high school, was the first person in my family to go to college, and was excited to start my life over," she said. "I had goals, focus, and drive—then BAM! This happened, and I was headed home with no direction on how to recover from the abuse or what to do next to move forward and refocus." As for Ashley's dad, once Ashley confronted him, he shifted the blame to Nicole, telling his family that Nicole was promiscuous (um, she was still a virgin and never had a serious boyfriend) and it had been a consensual affair.

When Nicole arrived home from college unannounced, her family knew something horrible must have happened to her, so she talked to them about it. Though Nicole never went to the police, her mom spoke to various members of her own church for counseling advice. This was hard because the ordeal rattled Nicole's faith in organized religion. And though Nicole wanted to be angry with God, she couldn't. "But I did lose faith in the church and ministry," she explained. "Before this happened, I would have described myself as a young adult excited about God, strong in my faith, and committed to the work of ministry. Not anymore."

From the moment Nicole moved out of Ashley's house, communication between Ashley, her family, and Nicole stopped. The last Nicole had heard, Ashley's mom wanted to literally shoot Nicole. Crippling insecurities and low self-esteem set in. Nicole felt dirty, undesirable, and unattractive. "I feared what relationships would look like for me in the future and the pain of having to share this past with a man one day if I were to ever get married," Nicole said.

Almost twelve years later, after the friends had drifted apart, Ashley found Nicole through social media and asked to hear her friend's entire story—gritty details and all. Interestingly, through all those years apart, both women had dreamed about the other, and in the dreams they were never angry. "It made me think that one day Ashley would hear my story and believe every bit," Nicole said. "It also made Ashley think that maybe there were a lot of details that her father was not sharing." Ashley soon revealed that many more sordid nuances had surfaced since Nicole had shed light on the abuse. Her dad had apparently lived a double life for years, with other abuse victims and several extramarital affairs. Ashley no longer has a relationship with her father, and her parents are divorced. Her father continues to live his life as a pastor.

The good news is that Nicole not only hit the reset button on her friendship, but rediscovered her faith. "Years later, my cousin invited me to his church, and I loved it. That was my way of telling God that I never left Him and was ready to get close to Him again," she said. "This journey gave me a greater passion to be a true, committed, and authentic follower of God."

What amazes me about this story is that Nicole lost so much during her friendship trials—so much more than someone to shop with or talk to on the phone. If you ask me, it's a freakin' miracle that the girl could get herself out of bed in the morning! At the time, Nicole lost her close confidant plus her dignity, faith in humanity, faith in God, respect for elders, trust, safety, and a sense of community. Incredibly, however, Nicole's story has a happy ending and shows us that not all friendship losses need to be forever. While some disappear for good, others can be refreshed with honesty, perseverance, and an open mind. Nicole regained her friendship, righted her path with God, and went back to school. What's more is that today she is married to a wonderful man and has two beautiful children. I couldn't be prouder of this woman and how she overcame her loss to find comfort again.

WHEN A FRIENDSHIP SPLIT IS FINAL

When a friendship ends, you can do your best to reach out to repair the situation, but listen, it's also possible that this loss is forever. No matter how much you apologize, your effort might not make it better. You should also respect the other person's need to end the relationship, even if it means no further contact. You may never know the real reason why your friend hit a wall with you, and the reasons might not make sense to you if you did know them. I can't tell you the number of times I've had a talk with someone after a conflict or misunderstanding, and when they told me their side of the story, I almost couldn't believe we were talking about the same conversation! I also think sometimes people just outgrow each other. Life-changing rites of passage like having a baby or getting married can make a friend feel second-best or no longer on the same page or life stage as you, whether this is an assumption or based on truth.

In the end, it doesn't matter because your friend no longer wants to be in a relationship with you, and you must accept this to heal. As your heart begins to mend, it can be a real challenge to learn to trust again and allow new friends and acquaintances to freely enter your life. It's natural to want to curl up under a blanket and binge on Netflix rather than put yourself out there, but you must.

When a friendship ends for good, the best way to process that loss is to grieve and mourn it for the heartbreak it has caused. Accept that your friend's decision to split is final, and if you have apologized, let it go if your offer to continue the relationship is denied. As a mourning ritual, it might help to write a letter to your friend that you never send. In it you can share memories, strengths, and even flaws—get your feelings out, rant and cry; and when you're finished, put it away until you're ready to throw it out, or hey, you can even burn it. Every few weeks after, check in with yourself about how you feel. You'll be surprised how much stronger you feel and what a better perspective you have when you gain distance from the situation.

From what Spirit shows me, all people are placed in our paths for a reason—and this includes all our friends, good and bad, past and present. Whether we allow them to help us grow and experience life is up to us.

Good Mourning

Think of a friend whom you are no longer close to. Did you do anything to provoke the split, and could you have done anything to change the outcome? Write a letter to this person and take responsibility for what you contributed to the situation. You don't have to mail the letter; you can set it aside or throw it away. The point is to get your feelings out. Putting your thoughts on paper will help you work through your emotions and gain a healthy perspective on what happened.

3

ON LOSING A SPOUSE TO SEPARATION OR DIVORCE

*G*rieving the end of a marriage can be one of the most pain-ful and heart-wrenching experiences that a person can go through. Without a doubt, Spirit says it is one of the heaviest hitters when it comes to everyday losses. Listen, I know that my own separation and divorce felt like a never-ending roller coaster of stomach-lurching emotions—one full of steep drops, sharp turns, and a huge feeling of relief when the ride was finally over.

Separating from a person you love, or once loved, has the potential to break your soul in half if you're not careful. After all, your spouse is a person who once meant the world to you, and now it may be a challenge to be in the same room together. You might feel painfully betrayed or disrespected depending on how your partner behaved toward the end of the marriage or how they chose to tell you that they wanted to move on. As a result, you may never trust the same way again.

During a divorce, you can grieve long and hard. You grieve the fact that you can't reach out for help or comfort to someone who'd always been there for you in the past. You grieve the loss of your identity as a spouse and member of your family, and what those roles meant to you. You might also mourn the realization that the person you'd spent your life with turned out not to be the person they seemed to be, and you may feel that the relationship was little more than a mirage. It hurts to know that the person you loved, and who you thought loved you back, may not have felt the same way. You may have thought that you'd found your soul mate for eternity, but when the relationship ended, you doubted how genuine your connection truly was. It's normal to question whether your feelings were ever real or if you were alone in them.

What's more, it's rare that a couple splits without each person showing an ugly or surprising side of themselves. As a friend told me, "You don't know someone until you divorce them," and I think that can be true. I will say, though, I'm proud of how I and my ex-husband, Larry, handled our divorce with respect and honesty, and how we tried hard to make the marriage work before we decided to end it.

MY EXPERIENCE WITH THE D-WORD

I met Larry when I was seventeen years old, and it wasn't until I hit age fifty that we realized we'd be happier separate than apart. We were bickering all the time, and it was very hard on our relationship. We were in therapy for about a year, then we separated for almost a year, and finally we decided to get a divorce.

Being on the road alone so much, I journaled a lot about how I was feeling and tried to understand when our relationship began to shift. I traced it to around 2001, which is much farther back than I had realized. Spirit says that our goal in life is to change, but Larry and I were growing in different directions at that time. I was also beginning to understand and embrace my gift and accept that working with Spirit was my soul's purpose. My grandmother was sick as well, which added to my hectic life. Larry kept his plate full too. Instead of addressing how all of these factors impacted our lives at home, we both stayed busy, which helped us ignore what was going on in our marriage.

I realize now that things fell apart, little by little, over the course of fifteen years. Gradual, subtle insults quietly but consistently eroded our relationship, and I just swallowed my feelings and kept on going. It wasn't until 2015 that we realized that we both weren't as happy in our marriage as we'd hoped to be. Both of us longed for things to be the way they were when we had first met, but we couldn't go backward. We wanted that playfulness and the feeling of being a family under one roof, but we couldn't get there no matter how hard we tried.

What I miss about marriage surprises me sometimes. Most of all, I miss our family dynamic and being part of a cohesive unit. I still grieve the memories we shared. They sneak up on me, in the middle of the night, and when the thoughts come, I can't go back to sleep. At my daughter Victoria's engagement party, we were all together, and I felt blue for what once was. I grieve my friendship with Larry too.

WHEN DIVORCE = DEATH

Even if you have an amicable breakup, a lot of people compare a divorce to a death, because it can feel that painful. After all, your partner is no longer part of your daily life, and that relationship has died. The end. Kaput. You've lost something you can't get back. Remember, a loss is a loss, and it all hurts. It's like how Spirit says:

whether a loved one dies suddenly to suicide or an accident or you've watched that person slowly decline from an illness over the years, the loss is equally poignant. The same goes for whether your marriage ends over five years or overnight.

At the end of a relationship, we try to justify the pain we feel by coming up with reasons why it hurts so badly, but in the end, Spirit says it doesn't matter. The relationship is over, and you're better off focusing on a brighter future. For me and Larry, there was no one, concrete reason why things ended. We simply changed and began wanting different things in our lives. Again, we also wanted what once was, the way things had been thirty years before, but that wasn't going to happen.

Mantra: I appreciate my ability to love and hurt, and I can learn and grow from both.

When you're in the thick of grieving a separation or divorce, Spirit says the key is to take it one day at a time, sometimes one hour at a time, and put your best foot forward as often as you can. Please realize that things really do happen for a reason, so even though your divorce might feel like the end of the world, it's likely the beginning of a new you. Try, too, to look at the positive side of your situation. If you're angry, think of the saying "Time wounds all heels"—and don't be afraid to laugh. Take care of yourself with healthy food and plenty of exercise, and remind yourself that you're a good person, a good soul. Find a purpose for yourself again, whether it's your job, your kids, or a new interest that your ex might not have encouraged. Pay it forward on a daily basis—buy a coffee for a stranger or hold the door open for someone—to keep your spirits high. Finally, because your identity has changed—you're not a spouse anymore—it's easy to feel you've lost your place in life. Create a new purpose for yourself, a little at a time.

SPIRITUALLY SPEAKING

A lot of people ask me whether God thinks divorce is a terrible blight on the soul, but you know, things happen. God doesn't want us to be unhappy. And Spirit wants us to love, honor, and respect ourselves the way that God intended; if a person stands in the way of that happiness for whatever reason, it's not against God's will for us to want to change that. If you stay in a relationship but are mean, bitter, sad, or angry, do you think that's how God wants you to live? Absolutely not.

Also remember that on the other side, there is no hatred or negativity, so in the afterlife, you may reunite with your spouse in a positive light. Chances are, there are karmic reasons that you were together for a certain time, but these will not be revealed to you until you are a soul in Heaven.

Spirit says that sometimes a divorce is fated because you're meant to develop other relationships and experience different types of growth. A part of me believes my divorce was part of my soul's journey. Together, Larry and I helped so many people by being public about our split on television; we showed others how to handle it with dignity and grace. When I was on tour, a man approached me with tears in his eyes and said that for years, he and his wife watched *The Long Island Medium* and wanted to thank me for being so emotionally open and honest about our divorce on TV. During one episode where Larry and I discussed what we were going through, the man said that he and his wife looked at each other and said, "That's us." They immediately started therapy together and are doing much better. The man said that they don't know what would have happened to them if it hadn't been for that episode, but they knew that they would not be as close as they are now.

So a part of me thinks it's my journey to help in this way, despite all the hurt that Larry and I felt throughout the process. Believing our divorce was purposeful has helped me deal too. I know the way we handled it was guided by Spirit. Look, I channel a lot of exes as souls who apologize for how they didn't love or respect a spouse on earth and have waited until they're dead to take responsibility for the choices they made that negatively affected their marriage. I believe Spirit has used me to help mitigate that. But you shouldn't wait until you're dead to make things right!

When a family isn't meant to split, however, Spirit will intervene. I once read a family who had a mentally disabled son named Shane who wandered out the back door of their home and drowned in the pool. Dad was babysitting at the time, and because it happened on Dad's watch, Mom had a very hard time forgiving him. The couple was on the cusp of divorce when they saw me. Yet when I channeled Shane's soul, he said that it was his father's soul's destiny to carry the burden of that death and not his mother's. If Shane had died under her care, she never would have been able to forgive herself. Channeling this message changed everything. Shane's parents are still together.

I believe that God gives us only what we can handle, and this includes how we mourn a divorce. For support, Spirit says to look for signs, symbols, and dreams that loved ones' souls send to provide comfort during the healing process. During my divorce, I dreamed about my grandmother's soul a lot and about fun things that happened when she was alive. Her soul would show me wonderful activities we did together, and I believe she sent these memories to comfort me because being with family has always made me feel secure. Dreaming of my grandparents brought me peace during a painful time; it was my grandmother's way of saying I'd be okay.

If you aren't experiencing spiritual intervention, then Spirit says you're likely too angry or sad for divine souls to penetrate your energy. Try to soften and remain open and aware of any strange, weird, or unusual things happening around you; these are often sent by Spirit. You can also pray to the Blessed Mother for support, as she's known for her compassionate, nurturing, and understanding presence. Deities from other faiths work just as well if they possess these traits.

I've learned a lot of lessons from my divorce, that's for sure. The biggest of all is compassion. I became a lot more empathetic through therapy and tried to look at things from Larry's side. And while this still didn't mend my marriage, I carried a more understanding heart into my daily life. I also learned to take responsibility for where I fell short. I realized that I became easily agitated and lashed out when I was unhappy. More than anything, I learned that nobody can make you happy but yourself. You have to own that.

With the divorce behind me, I can honestly say that I'm living my best life. Honest and truly. I am a strong and independent woman who does everything on her own, and I love it. I know Larry and I are both happier now that we have a different role in each other's lives, and that's nothing to be ashamed of. You must be true to your soul in order to embrace your most beautiful life on earth. Don't waste any time getting there.

Good Mourning

I believe it takes two people to make a marriage work, and two to make it fall apart. Think about one thing you may have done to contribute to your relationship's end and reflect on how you could have behaved differently. Soul search this topic in the quiet of your home or during a peaceful walk outside, then openly discuss this with a trusted friend or therapist. Your realization can't change the past, but how can you learn from it to enrich your future relationships?

4

ON LOSING FAITH

When you grieve an everyday loss, it's very common to feel slighted, overlooked, and betrayed by a higher power. After all, you're consumed by pain, you lose hope, and your faith bottoms out—who can blame you? You probably think it's a miracle if your prayers are even heard at all.

When you question God's role in your life during a loss of faith, it's important to remember that there are so many factors at work other than (1) your simply asking God for things to go your way and (2) His answering your request or not. Spirit tells me that God's MO is omnipotent, generous, and kind, but His plans can also seem complicated and unpredictable. Our circumstances play out on the basis of timing, the lessons our souls need to learn, destiny, free-will choices, and more. These factors can be out of our hands, within our control, neither, or both.

My friend Lori has a very strong faith, but years ago, her life and faith took a nosedive. Her son was having social problems, wasn't attending school, and was dabbling in drugs. Lori often wondered, *Why is God not protecting our family?* but these were her son's choices. God was allowing this young man to exercise his free will and then learn lessons from the decisions he made. When he was skipping baseball and hanging out with burnouts, it wasn't God's choice. It was the boy's.

WHAT'S GOD GOT TO DO WITH IT?

Losing faith ushers in a host of emotions. You feel deserted and forgotten. You feel resentment for unanswered prayers, or even worse, you suspect that God is choosing to answer your prayers with a "no." You feel surges of anger, a fear that years of belief in a higher power aren't real and you're made to play the fool. You feel duped and deceived for worshiping a God who claims to be with you but seems inconsistent—someone, or something, that He says He's not. You've put your energy, prayers, and love into serving God and now you feel that it was for nothing.

I've learned over the years from channeling Spirit that God is the number-one victim of our blame—there's that ugly word again—because we feel that we, or those we care about, wouldn't suffer if God were more in control, or loved us more, or listened better, or, or, or. We have a hard time believing that a random event would throw us a painful curveball, so we lose faith in God's power and devotion to us and wonder whether He exists at all. If we go to church, pray, and do our best to do good for others, we feel entitled to a blessed life. No wonder we freak when an everyday loss lands in our laps. We deserve better, dammit! It's easy to become defensive, depressed, and downright pissed over the seeming injustice of it all. God also becomes an easy target since we know that unlike a friend or family member, He won't shout back. In so many words, Spirit says to cut God some slack, here. He is with us always.

THE "ALL-OR-NOTHING" GOD

Some people turn from their faith immediately, and others stop trusting their belief system over time. Having faith requires that we believe in what we don't see, and given that we don't see progress or positivity when we experience loss, it makes sense that we stop believing in God. It takes faith to feel God, to see His signs, and to sense messages from the divine; if you no longer seek God out and trust that He's seeking you out, you will not be aware of these interventions if they come.

When a daily loss occurs, it's easy to see God as an "all-or-nothing" power, but the truth is, He operates in many shades of gray. If you lose faith, Spirit says you automatically assume that it's God who's doing the bad stuff, and that it's being done *to* you, rather than *for* you—which might not be the case. Perhaps your situation feels like a punishment, or even worse, a flip indecision. Yet I've learned from channeling Spirit that so many of our choices lead to the poor outcomes that define our losses, and other times, it's simply the way of life on earth. Bodies break, friends change, and finances bottom out. If your marriage falls apart, is it God's will, or did your spouse use his or her free will to cheat on you? Yes, you may have become hurt in a car accident, but did God tell you which route to take, or was that a free-will choice?

Our decisions, both good and bad, steer us down a path, and we are responsible for ourselves; God intervenes if it's His will to do so and in our best interest. That leaves all other choices up to us, and those around us. So yes, God is in control, but we are on this earth to make choices that affect our lessons, so *a lot* is up to us too.

PASS THE MUSTARD SEED

Sometimes the hardest thing is believing in God but not having faith that He is helping you and feeling that instead He is ignoring you or doesn't care about your welfare or the outcome of your daunting situation. This is when Spirit suggests you turn for inspiration to the Bible verse "If you have faith as small as a mustard seed, you can say to this mountain, 'Move from here to there,' and it will move. Nothing will be impossible for you" (Matt. 17:20, NIV). Given that a mustard seed is about one to two millimeters in diameter, it doesn't take much to move that mountain! This is preferable to losing faith, because once that's gone, you lose hope, and then love. And without love, you have nothing.

Mantra: I might have lost faith, but I can find hope and love in God's light.

What's cool about having a kernel of faith is that it has the potential to grow into a much larger belief system; the energy that you put behind a small amount of faith can build on itself and create the unexpected. A woman I know named Nicole always considered herself spiritual but didn't participate in organized religion as an adult, despite being raised Catholic. Just before her son Nate was due to enter kindergarten, he complained of leg pain and headaches and had low-grade fevers. Nicole dismissed these symptoms as growing pains, colds, and then later, the flu. She sent him to kindergarten on his first day, but just two days later, Nate's teacher along with the school nurse called Nicole to ask her to take Nate to the doctor. Nate's color was off to them, and they felt something was wrong. Nate's pediatrician ordered blood tests, one of which showed a very low hemoglobin level, which indicated that something was very wrong. When specialists ran additional tests, Nate was diagnosed with acute lymphoblastic leukemia.

While in and out of the hospital, Nate struggled with a great deal of pain caused by chemotherapy and steroid treatments. This prompted Nicole and her son to begin praying together, hoping to alleviate his suffering. "We prayed to Mother Mary the most," Nicole told me. "At first, I prayed because I hoped Nate would become distracted by us talking out loud or because he might believe it was helping and his brain would trick him into feeling better." Nicole had always been into meditation, and even though she and her son would breathe and meditate together at each clinic appointment, when the nurses inserted the needle into Nate's chest or spine for chemo, this was not solving Nate's pain issues. So Nicole decided to ask for help from a higher, more divine source. "I started with the only prayers I knew—the Our Father and Hail Mary," she told me, "and the Hail Mary stuck for Nate. I could hear him whispering it as I was saying it."

One night after a torturous treatment that left Nate crying in his sleep, Nicole considered the possibility that her son might not beat the cancer. *Oh Mary, please help me*, she thought. Nicole began praying the Hail Mary, over and over, almost like a meditative mantra. "I was paralyzed by fear and saw no other way to talk myself down," Nicole said. "I started to really panic. I was desperate for a miracle." Nicole was crying uncontrollably, when all of a sudden, she heard an unfamiliar voice in her head that patiently told her, "There is no reason to think your son will die today. One day at a time." Nicole describes the beautiful voice as quiet and calm—not her own. "I have a loud Italian, New Jersey voice," she laughed. "This voice was soft and feminine. It was almost a whisper, like a breeze blowing through a straw."

Nicole's faith began to grow, and Nate finished his treatment six months early. "His prognosis is excellent," Nicole said. Sometimes, Nate will still ask Nicole to pray with him when he's feeling anxious or experiencing residual pain from his illness. "Praying brings him peace," she said, adding that they still prefer praying to Mary. "I tell people that Mary's my homie. I believe she watches over moms and comforts us when we need it."

Nicole says she started her journey with a general belief in a higher power, but she now trusts that God and Mary look out for her family. "I also believe that angels walk among us—like Nate's school nurse, his teacher, and all the kind people who stepped in to support our family during this ordeal," she added. In fact, Nicole nominated her son's nurse for Pfizer's America's Greatest School Nurse Contest in 2018, and she won! With the prize money, the nurse bought Nicole's family, the teacher's family, and her own family orchestra seats to the play *Wicked* on Broadway. It's no wonder Nicole has rediscovered her faith. "We got the miracle we'd hoped for."

LOSING, FAST AND SLOW

It's possible to lose as much faith with a daily loss as you do with a death; Spirit says that the pace at which it disappears is simply different. You might lose your faith all at once when a loved one passes, but with everyday losses, because their painful impact can be cumulative over time, your faith could slowly dwindle. That said, daily losses also typically involve many losses at once, so it's easy to feel gobsmacked once a complete lack of faith hits. Daily losses can eat away at your beliefs so often that you don't realize how little faith you have left until it's too late.

The times I've lost my faith in God have mostly revolved around my gift. It isn't easy to channel for a grieving audience who isn't always grateful for what I tell them. Most of the time, the information I channel is welcomed with open arms. But once in a while, I experience a heckler or person so consumed by the anger stage of grief that I become their punching bag. During those times I feel like I'm being tested by God. Those are the moments when I have to spend extra time sitting in meditation and asking to be shown why I do what I do. I see flashes of people whom I've helped, and it's a reminder that not everything is perfect, and there will be ups and downs. If I ask God, *Is this what I'm supposed to really be doing?* His answer is always yes.

The next time you lose faith, remember that God has a bigger plan for you. It's okay to throw yourself a pity party today, but it can't be permanent. It's so easy to lose faith quickly, because we're a culture that embraces instant gratification above all else. Faith by its very definition, however, requires patience—and waiting is hard. If you realize the fact that your real purpose on earth is to grow a soul that lives *eternally*, you will find that having faith in God and His universal intentions means having faith in the long game. Right now, you are simply a soul having a physical experience in a human body. This is not your forever.

Sometimes the best thing that can happen to you is a loss of faith, because that's when God steps in with a sign that shows you how devoted He really is to you. I believe that everything happens for a reason, and this includes a loss of faith. You may have to hit bottom to rise again.

DOES LOSING FAITH HURT GOD'S FEELINGS?

When we're angry, feeling abandoned, and grieving the loss of faith, God gets it. He doesn't get mad when we lose our faith. Spirit says He understands and will always be there for us when we are ready. That is what I channel time and again. God is loving and forgiving. He doesn't pick and choose who to love and what to forgive. And if you restore your faith, God doesn't ask you to answer for this in the afterlife. It's only if you remain angry at God that you will need to discuss this with your guides during a life review process after you die. You will have the opportunity to see how things might have unfolded differently had you given God a chance. Or perhaps after you pass, your soul will become so overwhelmed by His glory that it will immediately ask for forgiveness for having turned its back on Him during hard times.

That said, God wishes for you to have faith despite what's going on. When I'm channeling and the room fills with gold and white light, I know that God is present. And He often says that even if you turn your back on Him, He will always be with you. He also likes to say that just because your prayers aren't answered doesn't mean they aren't heard. The only thing you can do is put your requests out there, place your future in God's hands, and feel grateful for what unfolds. Me? I turn to God a lot. He's always there for me, whether I'm loving and embracing Him or giving Him the cold shoulder because I'm cranky. It's the same for you.

When we've lost faith, we tend to point to the seemingly obvious ways that we feel God lets us down but not the little ways that He holds us up. We might hold God responsible for not protecting us from a life-threatening cancer but forget to credit Him for helping us find the doctor who helped bring about a remission. An illness may just be the result of an earthly body breaking down or poor choices, as with certain heart conditions or diabetes, while helping us find the right doctor is the act of a God who wants us to get better using the tools He has created on earth.

It's hard to predict what makes one person run toward their faith during a difficult time and another run away from it. Some of us have a stronger faith than others—it's that simple. Others have no more faith in humanity, perhaps after doctors or family members let them down, so they turn to the divine; God is thought to be the ultimate source of answers, after all. In my experience, I've found that those who don't make a habit of going to church, praying regularly, or engaging in other faith-driven practices are more prone to turning from God and losing faith.

Spirit says the best way to restore your faith is to go back to basics. Go back to church, say a prayer, admire a sunset, ask for a sign, and marvel at the glorious universe around you. You can be as angry as you want at God, but please don't lose your faith forever. You can be unhappy with Him and still have faith; you might simply need to set it aside while you grieve. When you are ready, you will realize that it was not God who let you down. Try to surrender to Him and simply trust that His bigger plan is not only in motion but worth the wait.

Good Mourning

The next time you feel ignored and abandoned by God, picture yourself sitting in a space filled with gold and white light, which is how I see God when He comes through during a reading. Do this in a place that makes you feel safe and close to Him, whether that's in a house of worship, your backyard, or barefoot in the woods. Spirit says that between the visualization and location, you will begin to relax into His presence. Once you feel your edges soften, say a prayer or simply talk to God and let Him know what's on your heart.

5

ON LOSING CONTROL

*S*pirit says that grief, by nature, is an out-of-control, uncomfortable time for even the most chill people out there. So when you are grieving everyday losses, you should prepare to feel powerless almost regularly. Daily losses and burdens such as losing a job or taking care of a child with special needs can make you feel as if you have no agency over your future or those you care about, as do losses such as infertility, parenting a child who's being bullied, custody battles, and being robbed. When a loss catches you off guard, Spirit says you are most prone to feeling out of control, but if I'm gonna level with you, I'd say that *all* the losses in this book will affect your perception of control, though some more than others, depending on how near and dear the subject is to your heart.

Loss challenges what you assume about life and forces you to face realities you hadn't faced before. This makes you feel out of control. Loss, in and of itself, is a control issue for everyone.

DON'T FIGHT A LOSING BATTLE

When it comes to grieving an actual loss of control, you have only two choices—to give in to the chaos or to fight against it, though Spirit says the fight for control is typically a losing battle. When things go on around you that have nothing to do with your choices, it's proof that other forces and decisions are at work—ones over which you have no authority and that you can't regulate (think car accidents and cheating spouses). That's scary. Losing control is especially confusing and painful in situations you don't understand. The world feels erratic and unpredictable. You don't know what's going to happen to you or the people you care about from one minute to the next.

A lot of stuff happens when you feel like you're losing or have lost control. Some people try to put the brakes on a situation and try even harder to control things in the future. You can become more controlling, agitated, and irritated instead of realizing there is little you can do. You might pick a fight, scream, or cry uncontrollably rather than ride out the situation to its end. Spirit says that sometimes, things just happen. The physical world isn't perfect—only Heaven is.

LET GO AND LET GOD

I believe that God gives us only what we can handle, which means most control issues can be mitigated by holding on to our faith. Sometimes we have to surrender to God and give Him the control. Loss is often a time to "let go and let God"—and also to allow spiritual beings like angels, guides, the souls of loved ones, and figures of faith do their thing.

I recently heard a story about a woman named Linda that is a perfect example of how God sends in reinforcements when we grieve the loss of control. Linda was in a situation in which she had no power, and the universe showed her that it had her back. God proved that her loved ones on the other side were ready to step in and take control in a situation where she could not determine the outcome.

Linda is the youngest of three siblings. Growing up, her two brothers were her idols. Even with an eleven-year age difference between her and her older brother Gerald, the two had a very close relationship. Gerald was her confidant, friend, and pseudo-shrink (he was also a therapist for a living). In February 2017, he began to feel ill. A regular walker, he was experiencing shortness of breath and couldn't trek as far as he once could. Despite seeing multiple doctors with multiple theories who offered multiple meds, Gerald grew worse. As he tried new treatments, Linda felt as if she couldn't help her brother in a way she wanted to. "I'd suggest random diagnoses for him to investigate, but then he'd shoot down my ideas," she said. "I felt really out of control in this situation, and I'm the kind of person who likes to take charge."

In May 2017, Gerald was finally diagnosed with amyloidosis, a rare disease caused by amyloid buildup in the organs. Amyloid is produced by the bone marrow and can sometimes leak into the body's organs, causing problems with the heart, liver, nervous system, digestive tract, and many other organs. There is no cure for the disease, but there are treatments that can ease the symptoms. One of them is a stem cell transplant, and Gerald decided to give this a go.

In the meantime, Gerald continued living as best he could, marking the days until the transplant. "Gerald had hope," Linda said. "We all had hope. Things were looking up." Linda made plans to fly to Baltimore to visit him after the transplant. She was also in constant contact with Gerald's daughter Sarah, and they joined an online amyloidosis support group. "We both like to find out as much as we can about tough situations," she said, "so joining this group and learning as much as we could and speaking with others gave us some semblance of the control we craved." Linda and her family stayed focused on the transplant, which was the closest thing to a cure.

Living in Florida so far from her brother didn't exactly make things easier for Linda. Toward the end of June, she woke up crying from a dream. "I have never had that happen," she said. "I woke my husband and told him immediately about it. It was so unusual, and I didn't want to forget it." In the dream, clear as day, Linda saw both of her deceased parents standing in a bedroom. Her mother was leaning against a night table, and to her left was her father, leaning against an armoire. They looked at Linda and then looked down at the floor as if to say, *Look down, look down.* In the dream, Linda tried to look down, but she couldn't see anything, at which point she woke up crying. "The dream was very vivid, so real. But I had no idea what my parents were telling me to look at, and this was upsetting to me."

A few days later, around 5:00 a.m. on July 1, 2017, Linda received a phone call from Gerald's wife, Leslie, who was crying, "He's gone, he's gone!" Linda's beloved big brother had passed away. The family was devastated. Linda flew to Baltimore to pay her last respects to this amazing, selfless, kind, and funny man. "He left an enormous hole in our lives," she said.

When she arrived at her brother's home, Linda asked Leslie what had happened—and specifically, where her brother had died. Leslie told her that around 4:30 a.m., Gerald had gotten up to go to the bathroom. Leslie got up too and went into the kitchen to make some coffee. She called in to Gerald and asked whether he was okay. Gerald said yes. She heard him walk back to bed—and then she heard a crash and the sound of Gerald moaning. Leslie ran to their bedroom and found Gerald unconscious on the floor. She immediately called 911 but she knew that Gerald was gone. Paramedics could not revive him.

Mantra: Life might feel out of control, but I am strong and resilient.

Linda asked Leslie to show her where her brother had fallen. In the bedroom, Leslie pointed to the very spot where her parents had stood in her dream and motioned for her to "look down." This astounded Linda. "He fell between a nightstand and an armoire," she said. "These were the exact same ones that were in my dream, that my parents were leaning against! Gerald did not die alone. My parents were with him."

Linda told her sister-in-law and the rest of her family about her premonition so that they'd feel comforted knowing that Gerald did not die alone. Linda feels strongly that her parents' souls were preparing her for his death, though at the time, she couldn't see it. When Linda told me this story, I immediately validated that these souls were with Gerald when he passed and that they wanted Linda to know they were there to greet him when he crossed over. It's true; he was not alone, and Linda was meant to share this story with others.

A few days later, after the funeral, Linda experienced a series of dreamlike visitations from her brother's soul. It's funny, because when Gerald was alive, his favorite saying was "Keep the lines open"—as in, the lines of communication—and this is exactly what he was doing! In one dream, Gerald was sitting on a stool on a stage, saying over and over, "I'm okay, I'm okay, I'm okay." Their parents were in the background with him, and then Linda woke up. A few weeks later, Linda had another dream in which Gerald called Linda on the phone to say that he was fine and that he "sees everything." To me, this meant that Gerald was addressing any residual fear of Linda's that he was potentially not at peace and wanted to reassure her that his soul is around her always, loving and guiding her just as when he was in a physical body. In her final dream, Linda saw Gerald walking down a street. "I ran to him, hugged him, and he hugged me back. I felt so peaceful," she said. "We looked at each other, and he just smiled and disappeared." It's very common for souls to appear in dreams without saying a word like Gerald did in this last visit; it requires a great deal of energy to even produce a hug or smile. Gerald is clearly an evolved soul.

When Linda thinks about her visitations, she's comforted knowing that her family is together on the other side and can both view and protect her life from afar. When Linda's dreams began, she said that she definitely felt she had no control over helping her big brother during his illness and being as supportive as she'd have liked. She also felt a lot of guilt over this, plus the fact that she was living in Florida while he was in Baltimore during his illness. Yet once her successive dreams ended, Linda felt the control gradually return to her life. "Looking back, I realize that you can't control every aspect of your life, especially when it concerns others—not to mention tragedies like illness or death. Life is full of kinks, and to navigate these roadblocks, you have to relinquish control and go with the flow," she said. "As it turned out, needing to feel in control the way I did proved unnecessary. Gerald showed me that he, my parents, and God were making sure that I knew that everything occurred exactly as it was meant to."

GRIEF FOR CONTROL FREAKS

Grief of all kinds—whether from a sudden, tragic death or a common, everyday loss—causes you to feel as if life is spinning out of control. It's a real "stop the world, I want to get off" moment, or perhaps even a series of them. If you consider yourself a controlling personality, the clumsy nature of grief is going to throw you for a big-time loop. It will drive you completely bananas that you cannot control your emotional outbursts. It will make you feel nuts if you aren't moving through the five stages of grief in order. You'll feel pain outside your comfort zone and be unable to stop yourself from crying in the cereal aisle of the grocery store. This is your hell.

When it comes to grief, the biggest problem for people who like to control their world is that mourning a loss is messy, disorganized, and seems to be a process with a mind of its own. You can't compartmentalize grief and get through it when you have the time and headspace for it. It sneaks up on you. Grief is in control, not you. A lump in your throat will catch you off guard and force you to feel your feelings more often than you'd like, in environments you'd rather avoid, and with people you'd never consider opening up to at any other time. Your plans will change depending on how you feel, and your language will change as you share how hurt you are with anyone who listens. Your clothes will change when you can barely get dressed in the morning, and a burst of tears will fog up your Ray-Bans when you're driving and need to see the road ahead. Nothing is predictable about grief, which makes it a double challenge for control freaks.

If this is you, then Spirit's advice is that you simply take your unexpected losses one day at a time. Accept that the pain of daily losses will sneak up on you, and that you must take each one in stride or else the grieving process will last even longer than you'd like. Admit that it's impossible to control the discomfort that comes from unmanageable sorrow and do your best to feel your feelings while waiting for them to rise up, calm down, and eventually pass.

SO WHAT CAN YOU CONTROL?

You can't control what it feels like to lose control, but Spirit says that it's human nature to try our best to do this (even if we don't succeed). This usually takes one of two routes. When losing control causes you to feel helpless and vulnerable, you may never want to let whatever caused this to happen, happen again, so you'll try to control things that happen to you or control your environment or relationships to keep things in the status quo. That's one option. The other is to just throw up your hands because you think bad things will happen to you no matter what you do. You might stop trying to make yourself feel better from whatever loss caused you to feel out of control, stop looking for ways to improve your situation, or completely give up on coping.

Spirit says a better choice is to find things that you can control and revel in those moments. You can control only yourself, which includes what you do, think, and feel. You can control your spiritual growth. You can take care of yourself and make the best choices you can every day. No matter what loss you face, your thoughts, beliefs, and attitudes are always yours.

Spirit is a big fan of having positive control over your life. Because free will is such an instrumental part of our experience on earth, and key to learning lessons, the souls that guide us don't always say that we should surrender *everything* to God. Yes, you should absolutely lean on God to give you the strength, perseverance, and endurance that will carry you through a fire. But putting one foot in front of the other, and walking through the flames, is entirely up to you. For instance, if you have an alcohol problem, Spirit insists that you do everything you can to get control over this. It's the same thing with diet and exercise, if you are at an unhealthy weight or suffering from heart disease. Spirit doesn't want you to feel helpless, but they need you to own your choices, grow from mistakes, and make wise decisions that yield a meaningful life on earth.

If there's an upside to losing control, Spirit says, in so many words, that losing control is an opportunity to check yourself before you wreck yourself. The next time you feel out of control, rather than spin out, stop and consider whether you can do something to make things better. Perhaps you can use the unwieldy moment to ground yourself in prayer, count your blessings, or remind yourself of those who support you. Remember, grief affects everyone, just in different ways. We're all in this daily loss game together, and we're all doing the best we can.

Good Mourning

Think of a time you felt you were either losing control
or out of control, and then received a sign from a loved
one—a coin, a familiar smell, a comforting dream—that
reassured you that everything would be okay. Take a
moment to thank God and Spirit for sending it, and the
next time you receive a sign, go one step farther to covet
this. If you see a message on a license plate, take a photo;
if you find a quarter, save it in a special box; if you see a
cardinal outside your window, put some seed out to invite
it back. Soon you'll be surrounded by gentle reminders that
Spirit is always with you, and you'll encourage the universe
to send more of these beautiful gifts.

6

ON LOSING YOUR HEALTH

Spirit has told me that when God designed us, He created physical, emotional, and spiritual bodies that were intended to be kept in balance to maintain good health. If just one of these components is out of whack, you might suffer in your body, mind, and/or soul because the whole system has been knocked off course. So when the disequilibrium arises because of an illness or injury, you not only feel its physical ramifications of, say, pain or disability, but also emotional issues like the frustration that comes with adopting new routines to suit your condition and spiritual problems such as not trusting a God who allowed you to become sick or injured in the first place.

When you lose your health, then, you might grieve some of the losses we've already discussed, like a loss of control or faith, plus a multitude of others like a loss of freedom, safety, or your identity. You grieve the life and abilities you once had—regardless of whether your condition is temporary or permanent. You also grieve a sense of self that's been lost. If you have a chronic diagnosis, it's hard to digest that there may be no cure for your illness and only symptoms to manage. You might also grieve past hopes or dreams that no longer fit your new reality. Battling illness can become truly life-altering, especially if you relive the grief process every time you experience a new symptom. Just introducing a new routine or using new equipment like a walker or brace can trigger a kind of trauma or stress response that is hard to shake.

I GET KNOCKED DOWN . . .

Trust me, I know what it's like to be floored by an injury. In June 2018, I was on tour in Honolulu, Hawaii, for a live show on my fifty-first birthday. I was standing by the shoreline at Waikiki Beach when a wave knocked me over. The surf and rip current are very strong there, and very different from what I was used to on Long Island! The force of the ocean was so powerful, in fact, that I almost drowned. The effects weren't just physically painful but emotionally terrifying and traumatic. What's crazy is that I initially was headed back to my room to get ready for my birthday luau but decided as I was getting into the elevator to turn around and hang out a little longer with the rest of my gang down by the water. Then, just like that, the wave hit—game over.

My knee really hurt, so when I finally had a day off during the tour, I flew home for tests and learned that, sure enough, I had torn my ACL, which is one of the knee's major ligaments. I scheduled surgery for a few months later. It was excruciating to stand on my leg, much less do any of the activities that were once part of my daily routine. For six months, I couldn't wear heels (nothing short of a catastrophe for me!), ride a bike, or exercise. This last one was particularly hard because I used to train six days a week, and now I couldn't use a treadmill, do squats, or lunge my way to a fit body. Simple things that other people take for granted, such as driving, getting dressed on my own, and sitting on a toilet became a real challenge for me.

After surgery, I worked hard to rehabilitate my knee, but still, to this day, if I sit for a long time, I sometimes have a hard time standing up. Let's just say that it took me more than a year and a half to do one freaking jumping jack! And now, although the knee has basically healed, my posture is different, which is affecting my back; so I'm trying to work through that to rebuild *those* muscles.

I know that I should feel relieved that my leg and knee are technically "fixed," but it's hard sometimes. I have to consciously tell myself that it's going to take time to accept a new normal and that I have to be patient. So I can relate to the frustration, defeat, and overall annoyance that clients feel when they grieve the loss of their health. When a body is injured as dramatically as mine was, you can't help but think, *Why is this happening to me?*

IS ILLNESS IN THE CARDS?

Some spiritual folks feel that we choose our bodies and illnesses before incarnating to earth, but honestly? I'm on the fence about this. I believe that some people are born with illnesses because they're meant to learn from them and affect the people around them based on how they cope with and navigate their conditions. Meanwhile, I think that others make free-will choices, perhaps with diet or by making risky decisions, that cause their bodies to become ill or get injured in the first place. And while your soul does not predetermine that someday you'll become a heroin addict or contract HIV, if you choose to turn that story into one of hope, healing, and inspiration, you are learning a lesson that comes from a positive, free-will choice. I'm shown that this is a decision that will be rewarded with soul growth on the other side. Remember, it's how you choose to live on earth that determines your soul's growth and life's happiness. As for death, I am shown that this is predetermined; when it's your time, it's your time.

When Spirit refers to illness, they encourage us to always take better care of ourselves. And they like to offer guidance as to why clients are feeling the way they do. If you can be doing something more, Spirit will let you know, whether it's time to change your medication, try certain vitamins, or find an acupuncturist. What Spirit doesn't say is that the body breaks, *la-di-da*, and that we should strictly focus on our soul's growth during this time—that we are souls, first, living in human bodies. Nope. Even soul growth is a choice. Instead, Spirit values our bodies and emphasizes that we have them for a lifetime and need to take care of them. If you let the body's pipes leak and roof cave in, it will lose its value and crumble to the ground. Your soul's "home" won't be able to help you live your best, and most meaningful, life.

Acceptance plays an essential role with any loss, but it's especially important with illness. It's so easy to get stuck in how much you've lost to an illness that you forget to appreciate what you still have. Again, I get it. But you must accept, and celebrate, the pieces of yourself that are unchanged. Perhaps even with your illness, you're still a wonderful mother, daughter, friend, or wife. And with this in mind, you must stay focused on who you are now and how to learn, grow, improve, and even change the situation you're in.

Yes, I just said *change*—as in heal. Though a broken body may feel unfixable, Spirit says that in actuality, your body is constantly trying to heal and return to a new state of equilibrium, or homeostasis. Whether it's through Western, integrative, holistic, or energetic techniques, you can always do something more for your body, mind, and soul to help you find balance.

ALWAYS LOOK ON THE BRIGHT SIDE OF LOSS

A big part of healing, and arguably the most challenging for most people, is maintaining a positive perspective while you're ill or injured. Believe it or not, there are positive ways to view the loss of health. Because of your condition, you might make new friends and acquaintances, appreciate experiences you hadn't before, and see people for who they truly are.

This last one is bittersweet, as it can be a painful realization when you lose friends or family support during a health struggle, but ultimately you need to acknowledge that you will heal faster without them. It's a real eye-opener to recognize who the kind helpers are in your life versus those who can't be bothered. Support may come from the least expected places—a group of new friends from your regular breakfasts at the local bagel shop, an acquaintance whom you happen to always bump into at the pharmacy, or an old friend who suddenly reenters your life at the right time. These positive twists aren't a coincidence, and Spirit wants you to embrace them for the fortunate, divine guidance they are.

You might also choose to believe that your illness is happening for a reason. Perhaps the fact that your spouse left while you were dealing with cancer was a blessing in disguise. Maybe the fact that you're ill from a moldy home was meant to move you into a new neighborhood where you'll meet a new best friend. I definitely believe that the wave that knocked me over was serendipitous, and the fact that I was down for the count while trying to rehabilitate my knee was determined by God. Remember, I was about to head up to my room when something told me to turn back and head to the shoreline. I wasn't even supposed to be there!

The truth is, I was struggling with a lot at the time. I was making reckless financial choices by planning big trips and spending too much money on clothes, because I was having a hard time with the fact that Larry had started dating again during our separation. I wasn't paying attention to that giant wave when it came crashing toward me, just like I wasn't paying attention to what I should have been doing to heal myself and stay focused on the positive stuff in my life while going through my divorce. I was running away from my pain rather than facing it head-on. I know that my injury was God's way of saying, *You must take a more thoughtful look at your life and make better choices. No more rash decisions based on things you have no control over. Slow down. Step back. Relax. Love and respect yourself.* I've always believed that things happen for a reason, and keeping this in mind helped me get through my injury. I was literally knocked down and forced to stand up again on my own. How's that for an obvious message?

WHEN LOSS BRINGS YOU TO YOUR KNEES, LOOK UP

When you're suffering during the loss of your health, I suggest looking to spiritual role models for both guidance and a lift to your spirit. I like praying to Saint Jude, the patron saint of desperate and lost causes, as well as the archangel Raphael, who's a supreme healer in the angelic realm and whose main role is to guide, support, and heal in all matters involving health. In fact, Raphael means "God heals" or "He who heals" in Hebrew. His job is to guide you toward comfort and recovery. This might include "showing you" encouraging license plates, sending you messages in songs on the radio, guiding you to books related to your health crisis, prompting gut intuition about your doctor's next steps, and even showing you green lights that symbolize healing. These are all ways that Spirit, especially angels and saints, communicate when you're ill.

When you're having a particularly bad day, perhaps it will help to remember that you will not be in your imperfect body forever. When the soul leaves the physical body, you will become free of its burdens and heaviness. You will leave illness with the body, feeling peaceful and light. In times of need, close your eyes and imagine what this will feel like. Meditating on this feeling will mentally transport you to a heavenly space that will temporarily free you of worldly sorrow.

Spirit tells me that those who suffer more on earth have the potential to graduate to a higher level in Heaven, because they are given more opportunities to learn lessons from their grievances. Empathy, patience, kindness toward others—these are all lessons that often revolve around illness. Your illness might not only bring you lessons but offer an opportunity for those around you to learn as well. I'll never forget doing a live show in the Washington, DC, area, where a husband's departed soul apologized to his living wife for the losses that had occurred around his illness—Alzheimer's disease. So much about this debilitating condition is related to loss for both the person who is sick and the caretaker who helps. Those with the condition deal with the loss of their identity and suffer from memory loss and other cognitive issues; they also have to cope with losing a sense of agency and responsibility when they face problems like wandering and getting lost, have trouble handling bills and with repeating themselves, take longer to complete normal daily tasks, and have to deal with personality and behavior changes. Caregivers also feel loss as their loved ones change and eventually may no longer seem like the person they knew and loved.

When I channeled this man's soul, he explained that while he was ill, he often complained and threw food at his wife and became angry at what she was able to do or not do for him. He learned the lesson of empathy on the other side and apologized, saying it was the illness, and not him, that had made him act the way he had. He told her that he loved her and assured her that she had done everything she could have done, above and beyond what was needed. He thanked her for the first time since he had become ill and died, and the message was a Godsend. This man's wife had been feeling guilty that she hadn't done enough for her husband. She worried that if she'd done more, then he wouldn't have been so upset all the time. Now that he had passed, she also felt guilty for living her life again and enjoying herself without him. But his soul was there to encourage her to embrace life with happiness and joy. He erased the grief that both of them had felt by channeling through me.

BETWEEN PAINFUL MOMENTS, THERE IS GRACE

Perhaps because illness can feel so all-consuming, so entirely defeating and without answers, Spirit often allows for spectacular spiritual events to occur when we're in the thick of it. These might include meditative awakenings, visits from loved ones' souls, and glimpses of Heaven that remind us that our guides, angels, and loved ones are always trying to make us smile. They reassure us that life marches on and despite all our setbacks, the extraordinary still has the potential to occur. And when we're grieving the loss of our health, God is always there.

I know a woman named Kelly, whose young daughter Olivia battled a malignant brain tumor at the same time that she herself was battling cancer. The one-two punch was because of a genetic mutation that Kelly carried which she had inherited from her father and passed on to two of her three children. When Olivia was ill, Kelly's Aunt Carol taught herself to meditate by going into her heart, breathing deeply, and healing old wounds. As she put this into daily practice, an image of a cave came to her. Carol felt safe imagining herself inside the cave, the same way that she felt safe inside her own heart.

After Carol received the image of the cave, she sketched what she saw in her mind's eye and then created an incredible paper collage image of the cave. She shared her meditative experience and special artwork with those closest to her and believed that the cave was a place for all to imaginatively gather in their own medi-tations. She said that they could go there individually or as a group when they needed to be supported in any way. About a year after Carol's mediation, Olivia passed away at the age of five.

Just two months before Olivia's passing, while Olivia was still fighting for her life, Kelly had had a tumor removed, and a biopsy of it showed that Kelly had a kind of soft tissue cancer. A sec-ond scan after Olivia's death then showed a new, suspicious spot in Kelly's liver, which doctors suspected was metastatic disease. Kelly left her oncologist's office feeling overwhelmed with emo-tion. She was already battling guilt and depression over passing on the genetic mutation that had taken her daughter's life, and now she had two additional cancer diagnoses of her own to deal with.

As Kelly stepped into the shower the morning after her doc-tor conducted that second scan, she felt flooded with fear. She was afraid of the cancer spreading, afraid of putting her fam-ily through more hell, and afraid of the worst possible outcome:

death. As the water ran down Kelly's face, she closed her eyes and found herself in the cave that her Aunt Carol had visited during meditation.

And then the unbelievable happened—a reassurance from the other side that Kelly would be okay. "In my mind, I was sitting in the cave with my legs crossed looking out at the distant mountains," she said, "when two small arms wrapped around my waist from behind. I knew immediately that it was Olivia's soul. Tears ran down my cheeks. I felt loved, safe, and knew that all would be okay no matter what. In that moment, the cave became my own safe space, and ultimately a place to meet my daughter's soul."

This experience showed Kelly that visitations can happen when you are fully awake. "I knew about the signs from loved ones, like feathers, pennies, music, and for Olivia, rainbows," she said. "But I had never experienced a true visitation, especially one that wasn't in a dream."

As Kelly and her husband walked into the hospital to have her biopsy completed, she realized in that moment that no one had a clue how overwhelmed she was feeling. How could they? They didn't know Kelly's cancer journey, and they certainly didn't know she had just lost her daughter a few months before. Kelly held her breath, as the nurse instructed, while the long needle was inserted, numbing the path to her liver. A sudden pop-feeling startled Kelly as her eyes began to well with tears. "I wasn't aware that the liver capsule would feel that way," she said. "It was my breaking point, and my tears were uncontrollable. My heart rate soared, as I tried to catch my breath from probably the hardest cry that I've cried since Olivia's passing."

The next morning, Kelly was in the shower again and relieved that the biopsy was complete, but she anxiously awaited the re-sults. As she stepped out of the shower and reached for her towel, she saw herself back in the cave. This time she was standing in it and felt a gentle nudge from behind her to move forward and out of the cave.

"I knew it was Olivia's soul and wondered what the message was," she said. "I remember feeling afraid that beyond the cave could have been a steep cliff, but instead there was a plush, grassy hill. I lay down on the hill, arms spread wide, sun on my face, feeling free. This experience was powerful. This was like a daydream that we so often have, but one that I couldn't possibly create on my own." Kelly said that she knew Olivia was bringing her comfort at a time of dis-ease. "My daughter's gentle nudge was a message to get moving," she said. "She was telling me to get out in the sunshine, enjoy this planet's grassy hills, and live life. There's still so much to see. All is well."

Mantra: I might be down, but I'm not dead.

About a month later, Kelly agreed to meditatively meet Carol in the cave. Carol was in her home, and Kelly was in hers. Olivia's room had become Kelly's refuge—a quiet, sacred space to just be—so she sat on Olivia's bed to join Carol in spirit. As Kelly closed her eyes and focused on breathing into her heart, she was immediately at the cave. This time, she was outside, sitting on a rock, legs crossed, overlooking that grassy hill below her with incredible mountains in the distance. "Olivia came bopping around the corner and plopped herself down on my lap just as she normally would have done," she said. Her daughter's soul had hair again (Olivia had lost all her hair during cancer therapy) and looked happy and healthy. "We giggled, and then she took my hand and led me around the corner, just outside of the cave. I stopped, as there stood thousands of people in the distance among fields of grass and gorgeous flowers." She believed Olivia was showing her various souls in the afterlife and the beauty of Heaven.

Months later, Kelly had one final meeting with Olivia outside the cave. At this point, she was undergoing a second biopsy as the results for the first one had been inconclusive. In Kelly's mind's eye, she and Olivia rolled down a grassy hill sideways, having the best time. "We talked about meeting here in this place. Our visit was fun, lighthearted, and full of joy," Kelly said. "It has become clear to me that we are connected always, no matter where we are."

The cave that Kelly's Aunt Carol visited was clearly designated as a space for their family to receive guidance and feel love from the other side. All experiences at the cave happened quickly and in the meditator's mind's eye. As a result of these phenomenal encounters, Kelly's faith has become stronger than ever before as her belief system has expanded. "Part of any illness journey or the passing of a loved one is the loss of what was," she said. "I believe we're all capable of receiving messages if we have an open heart in a safe, sacred space."

Even when you're barraged with illness, taken down by injury, and questioning whether it's worth hobbling into another day, God and Spirit insist it is. They, and all of your loved ones on earth, need for you to keep pushing and loving yourself enough to find the healing you crave.

Good Mourning

No matter what your diagnosis, Spirit wants you to live the best life you can and embrace each day as if it's your last. Sometimes our medical experts deliver prognoses that get us down, yet nobody but God knows exactly how, when, or why an illness will progress.

Write down the last bit of discouraging news you heard from your doctor and how it made you feel, and then tear it to shreds. So much about how you overcome or succumb to disease has to do with what *you* want the outcome to be. Have faith. And then make yourself living proof of that determination to thrive. When you're feeling your worst, self-care falls by the wayside. Go get a blowout, pedicure, or buy yourself a cozy new robe and slippers. You'll feel better for it!

7

ON LOSING INDEPENDENCE

Losing independence and freedom can come from a burdensome situation, like when you become a caretaker for someone who is ill, or from a joyful one, like when you lose your independence as a newlywed or a new mom because you can't go out like you used to and are suddenly beholden to another person.

When you lose your independence, you naturally grieve and feel a cascade of emotions. You can feel powerless, anxious, fearful, unsure, and hesitant. And though it's the last emotion you want to admit, sometimes you can also feel bitterly resentful of a person or situation for creating your loss of independence. Spirit says that the heart of this grief isn't necessarily selfish but comes from a fear of missing out on life, and even a vague awareness of your mortality. If you had all the freedom in the world, after all, you could go to unlimited movies, buy season tickets for your favorite baseball team, and plan a vacation to Fiji. Who wants to give all that up, right?

Try to remember, however, that on a soul level, we are connected to our loved ones for eternity. Though you may not want to deal with a loss of independence because of another person on this plane, Spirit says you're privileged to care for those who share soul bonds. My aunt actually modeled Spirit's lesson when she cared for my grandparents, who died five years apart. She loved being by their side and giving back to them for all they'd done for her when they were able. When my grandparents passed, my aunt was so distraught that she saw herself as an orphan. She essentially lost her purpose, and regaining her independence didn't feel like a blessing. You never know: Spirit says a situation like my aunt's might have been fated before her and my grandparents' souls came to this world. The lessons one learns from a loss of independence can be trying but life-changing. They will forever mold your spirit, long after the situation has passed.

THE GOOD, THE BAD, AND THE UNFORTUNATE

When I was a young parent, my life revolved around my children. When Larry, my oldest child, was still a baby, just the simple act of taking a shower was a serious feat! I'd put Larry in his play-pen in front of the TV and sneak off to hit the shower. I'd then wait until he was napping to blow-dry my hair. At some point in between, I'd get dressed. I'd usually have to call my mom, who lived next door, to run over and watch Larry while I made myself something to eat. I'd have emotional breakdowns on the regular because I was exhausted, smelly, and hungry. And even though I enjoyed being a mother, life as I knew it had become interrupted, and I deeply struggled with the loss of my independence. I also know a lot of fathers who resent having to give up their freedom to co-parent or help mothers take care of their family. This is one reason that therapists say the first year of a child's life can cause an exhausting strain on a marriage. Each person is forced into a new, grown-up role that alienates them from the freedom they once loved.

You can also lose your independence all on your own, like when you are ill, have been in an accident, or grow older. You might not be able to drive or bathe without assistance anymore. I think of my maternal grandmother, Gram, and how upset and frustrated she'd get when she could no longer drive because of her age—she couldn't shop for groceries or get her hair done on her own, so she felt hemmed in by other people's schedules and acutely aware of how the passing years affected her life skills. I'm sure that on some level, as Mom was chauffeuring her around, Gram realized that when you age, your children become your parents. This is frustrating on both sides. Spirit says that when you've lost your independence and are being cared for by another to remember what that other person is going through. Have compassion. Practice empathy. Stretch yourself. You have every right to grieve, but it's not solely about you. Everyone has lost some independence.

WHERE DID YOUR LIFE GO?

When someone believes they've lost their independence by taking care of a person who then passes, the departed soul will always come through when I channel to thank that person in the physical world for putting their lives on the back burner. They're grateful for the sacrifices and recognize how much has been set aside for their wellbeing. It's hard to see this in real time, though, especially when the person you're caring for suffers from dementia or is a child and not mature enough to realize how their situation affects others.

I know a strong and refreshingly candid woman named Carla, whose daughter Ellie has medically intractable epilepsy with frontal lobe disorder. Carla has endless love for her child, but she struggles with how much of her own life she's sacrificed to be sure Ellie can live hers. Ellie was diagnosed when she was seventeen months old, and she's now sixteen years old, so Carla and her family have been dealing with this illness and related responsibilities for many years.

As Ellie's primary caretaker, Carla struggles enormously with how Ellie's care weighs on her daily energy, happiness, and routine. For instance, Ellie can't drive. "We live in a city without great public transportation, and Uber will no longer let kids her age ride alone, so she's completely dependent on me for getting around," Carla told me. Ellie also can't manage her own medication, so every day there is a ton of anxiety around making sure she has taken the right meds, at the right dose, at the right time. "This, of course, complicates things like sleepovers, camp, business travel for me, college, and eventually, independent living for her," Carla added. And although Carla and her husband have the financial means to hire some help so they are able to still travel and work, they do this with a lot of anxiety and interruption.

"My biggest fear is that things will never change," Carla confided, "and that Ellie will always be dependent on me. And not in a way that some passive, quiet, disabled adults are. Ellie thinks everything's fine. She is super vocal. She screams about not needing my help, but she does. That paradox is hard, and unless some brain surgery miraculously cures her, nothing is going to change, which means things are going to get much, much worse when high school ends. School and sports essentially serve as day care and let her lead a pretty normal life."

Carla has had to sacrifice a lot for Ellie. Caring for her daughter has made having a productive career difficult, because Carla always has to be available in case of any emergency, and that is very limiting. Carla says that her husband does not face the same limitations, but he would claim that he works harder to pay for a future when Ellie might not be independent.

As an example of how demanding her days are, Carla explained how they tried a ketogenic diet for three months to help reduce the number of Ellie's seizures. "It took six hours a day to prepare her food," Carla said. "I had to run everything through a computer program to get the nutrient ratio correct—four grams of fat for every one gram of protein and carbs combined. I had to weigh every ingredient to one-tenth of a gram. It wasn't like the commercial keto fad diet that so many people think they do. And after all that, the diet didn't help Ellie." What's more, Carla has traveled all around the country chasing different doctors and tests to try to establish whether Ellie would be a candidate for various surgeries (so far, she hasn't been), and she has visited multiple therapists to get Ellie psychological help.

Carla says that the best way to describe how Ellie compares with other kids her age is this: imagine taking an eleven-year-old and putting her in her junior year of high school. That's what it's like parenting Ellie. "Her executive function is very poor, so she can't set a goal and then break it down and move backward through all the steps it will take to reach that goal, even if the goal is as simple as meeting a friend at a restaurant at noon," she said. Ellie also has very little self-control, logic, or empathy. She can behave like a spoiled child, acting out in public places without regard for the people around her. This is especially hard for Carla because Ellie doesn't look disabled, so people sometimes stare at Carla like she's a horrible mother. Ellie has also walked away from the stove with the gas light still on, taken a thirty-minute shower without washing her hair, and is prone to wearing her clothes inside-out. She appears unable to connect cause and effect too, so she makes the same mistakes over and over and fails to learn from them, which is hard for Carla to watch. Anyone who speaks to Ellie would think she is much younger than she is.

This lack of independence has affected Carla's relationship with her other kids and her husband. She occasionally resents her husband because she's in charge of everything. He takes his turn doing things like overnights in the hospital when he can, but if you asked him what Ellie's prescriptions are and the doses, Carla doesn't think he could tell you. "He resisted support groups and the like early on and didn't want epilepsy to define her," Carla said. "That came from a good place, but ultimately it bit us in the rear because now disability is not part of her identity, which I think is a big part of why she doesn't understand her limits with things like college admissions." Carla has read tons of books on epilepsy and recommended them to her husband, who says he'll read them and then doesn't. He doesn't do any independent research and hasn't gotten involved with advocacy or support groups. All of this can make Carla furious.

To compound problems at home, Ellie's epilepsy is very hard on Carla's youngest son, who is three years younger than Ellie. He gets angry that she doesn't get punished the way he does. Ellie throws tantrums like a toddler, and he sees that, and although he knows he can't do the same, this still strikes him as unfair. Carla's oldest son, who's three years older than Ellie, used to feel the same way. "But now that he's nineteen, he gets that her life is always going to be a real challenge, and that it's hard on us, and we're all just doing the best we can," Carla said.

Ongoing drama with Ellie, her spouse, and her other children zaps Carla's energy and patience every day. This leaves little headspace for Carla to unwind on her own or go out with friends—not that she feels anyone could sympathize with her situation in a way that would help. "No one gets it," she said. "They say, give Ellie an Apple Watch to set medication reminders, or they'll tell me that all teenagers are disorganized." But Carla knows that Ellie is different—that she can't keep track of a watch, keep it charged, or remember what the watch alarm is supposed to remind her to do. "When people say things like that, what I hear is, 'I can't be bothered to even try to understand what you're going through,'" Carla added. "It can be isolating. Even people in my own family say stupid stuff like that."

Mantra: I'm freer than I think. Feeling trapped is a state of mind.

Carla's sense of lost freedom and independence mostly presents as resentment and the blues, as she grieves for the girl that Ellie could have been and the woman Carla could be without this unusual responsibility. To cope, Carla runs, goes to therapy, and probably drinks more beer than she should. She avoids situations that she knows will upset her, like attending church or going shopping with Ellie, and she avoids friendships with other moms who have daughters the same age because it's hard to watch the girls mature. "There are parents who say it all serves a purpose or that they learn more from their disabled kid than their kid does from them, and they wouldn't change a thing, but that is not where I am," she said.

When I heard Carla's story, Spirit relayed that for as limiting as her life is, Carla would benefit from focusing on what she *can* do with her family versus what she can't do on her own, and appreciate the time that she's spending with her child, as trying as it is. In fact, Spirit said that if Ellie weren't ill, their relationship wouldn't be as close as it is, and without going into detail, there are larger, karmic reasons for their interwoven relationship. Spirit honors family relationships, and they feel it's a good thing for Carla, in some ways, to devote the time she has to Ellie. They also noted how strong Carla is, and that this situation has redefined her life purpose. And while perhaps Carla is unable to help Ellie as much as she would like to, Carla can still help others in a similar position with everything she's learned about epilepsy. It's amazing that Carla works so hard for her daughter and could have given up a hundred times—but didn't.

TAKING BACK YOUR LIFE

If a situation causes you to lose your independence or freedom, even if it's for a noble or sometimes rewarding reason, Spirit says that you have to take care of yourself in the midst of it. The potential grief that will come of it will break down your spirit if you don't make time to unwind and separate yourself from the situation that burdens you. Spirit says that even small efforts will make a difference. Once a week, take an hour to get a pedicure or go for a walk. Spread out a blanket, take off your shoes, and lie in the grass on a sunny day. Movement and meditation, depending on whether you're feeling energized or depleted, will also ground you in the moment and help you take the beat that your mind, body, and soul desperately need. Find ways to refuel your joy as best you can, so that you don't feel you're entirely missing out on the life you want versus the one that you might feel has been unfairly thrust upon you.

Good Mourning

Do an activity that makes you feel free. Ride a bike down a hill. Go for a drive in a convertible with the wind in your hair. Meet a friend for lunch with no time limits on when you need to get home. The goal is to remind yourself of who you are and how it feels to live without constraints.

8

ON LOSING SAFETY
AND FAMILIARITY

Spirit says that when you lose a feeling of safety, you simultaneously lose a sense of familiarity—and vice versa. Feeling secure in a lifestyle, environment, or daily routine that you comfortably recognize is super important when you're hit with a loss of comfort and well-being. So many of the situations that we discuss in this book, from divorce to financial loss, can cause you to feel thrown into a world that no longer feels like yours. Of course, the loss of a loved one or of a pet, especially when the death is unexpected, will also provoke these feelings. All of these scenarios can cause you to feel like you're slogging through a weird dream or horrifying nightmare, or that you've been body snatched and are now living someone else's life. To lose safety and familiarity is to feel startled and on guard, day in and day out, so Spirit says to practice routines that help you replace feelings of vulnerability with those of self-assurance.

NOT SO SAFE AND SOUND?

Losing a sense of safety can especially occur with trauma, whether you are directly affected by a horrific occurrence or hear about one from others or through the media. Monumental events like 9/11, Hurricane Katrina, and mass shootings certainly impact those within the directly involved communities, but they also bring together people who learn about these tragedies on the news. Such mournful events are layered in loss, but Spirit says a feeling of unrecognizable insecurity is at the forefront. In fact, losing safety and familiarity reminds me of the lyrics from Carole King's song "I Feel the Earth Move": *I feel the earth move under my feet / I feel the sky tumbling down.* Of course, King is referring to how she feels around her big crush, which shows us that you can also lose stability during a positive event like falling in love. But for our purposes, losing safety can feel like the ground beneath you is unsteady and that you're losing your bearings, soon to fall into the center of the earth as the sky above you simultaneously squashes you into a million little pieces.

Feeling a lack of safety and familiarity after a trauma reminds me of a woman named Wendy who felt incredibly unsafe in her abusive home and dysfunctional family her entire life—that is, until a miraculous event caused her to reevaluate her awareness of divine protection.

Since Wendy was a young child, she endured "heaps of abuse, alcoholic rages, and lies directed at me," she said. Most of the evil treatment came from her mother, who is an alcoholic and a narcissist and has borderline personality disorder, though Wendy's enabling stepfather also contributed. "The evil and hurt they projected onto me is beyond my understanding," she told me. "I felt like a sick drug to my mother. She was always putting me down, smacking me, making me cry, and lying about me; it seemed to make her high. The more chaos, hate, and sadness that she could create, the better."

Wendy's family was wealthy and postured to the outside world, so to strangers her mother "was a beautiful mom with perfect clothes, a beautiful house, and an ideal life. Once the door to our house was shut, however, life was nothing short of a true nightmare." As her mother's favorite target, Wendy was told daily that she was ugly, fat, smelled, and had no friends. "If I told her I loved dogs, she'd say that dogs didn't like me," Wendy said. "When I was voted friendliest in the class, she told me nobody cared and that she had been the homecoming queen and I wasn't." If this weren't enough, Wendy's mom regularly accused her of stealing, lying, and breaking things around the house, and Wendy's stepfather believed these things.

Despite their wealth, Wendy's parents deprived her of a child's basic needs. Her mom never kept food in the house, and Wendy was forced to subsist on very little—"Thank God for Miracle Whip on toast." Because Wendy rarely received new clothes, she taught herself to sew so that she could patch holes in her clothes or sew new fabric onto her pants' hems to turn them into boot-cut jeans. She learned to hide anything or anyone she cared about—books, jewelry, crayons, even her younger siblings, whom she constantly protected from abuse.

"I had to survive any way I could," she said. "It was a cold, hurtful, and lonely life. I cried myself to sleep a lot, wondering whether anyone out there loved me." Because of Wendy's dark and heartbreaking upbringing, she constantly felt unsafe and found it hard to believe that she was being protected or guided by anything divine, especially God.

A few years ago, Wendy decided to end all contact with her family to protect herself and her two young children from continued abuse, which only compounded the multitude of losses she had endured over the years. "This split was the hardest thing I've ever gone through. It isn't easy to grieve people who are still alive but not healthy to be around. The pain is soul crushing. It feels like a weight is pressing on your heart at all times," she said.

Around that time, Wendy was living in a suburb north of Chicago with her husband, Nick, and children, James and Emma. One day, she went for a drive with the kids, who fell asleep in their car seats. She parked the car in a lot off a busy road and read a book while they napped. She often kept a book in the car for this reason—reading in the front seat until they woke up. When her son stirred, Wendy realized her quiet time was over and began driving out of the lot to head home.

Just then, Spirit got Wendy's attention. "I was at the stop light waiting for the green arrow to turn left," she said, "and just as the arrow came on, and I took my foot off the brake to drive, something or someone told me, 'Hand James a book.'" Wendy said she heard the voice in her head, almost like a knowing. "I didn't think too hard about this, so I went with what I felt."

Wendy put her foot back on the brake instead of turning left and grabbed the book off the car floor. Seemingly out of nowhere, an eighteen-wheeler barreled through the intersection, right in front of Wendy's car. Coming off the highway and driving very fast, the driver never saw the red light and went straight through the intersection that Wendy would have been turning into seconds before. "Had I turned left at that light, we would have been hit hard, T-boned, and dead," she said. "I put my car in park and just cried a deep, deep sob. Someone from above saved our lives that day."

Since then, Wendy says that she has a newfound faith in the protection of God and loved ones on the other side. Given her past, she couldn't believe that "someone, somewhere wanted me alive. Someone loved and cared for me enough to save us from that crash. It gave me hope to keep moving forward, to keep trying my best and that life is a blessing." Her faith in God has been restored, as has her will to live. What's more, Wendy said that she's made a pact with herself to give back, so now when she feels sad or thinks about the abuse she has endured, she volunteers. Each time she cries, she takes a gift to someone, compliments a stranger, or pays for someone's coffee. "I try to walk a more thankful path and be a light to others," she said. "I fight the sadness and hurt with laughter and love. I want to turn my story into a positive one."

When Wendy told me this horrendous yet moving story, I had a strong feeling that a grandmother figure saved her, and Wendy validated that the mother of her biological father, who lost custody of Wendy as a child, was on the other side. Wendy never knew her, but she could still be a strong guardian. "Whoever it is, I am so thankful," she said. "They saved my babies' lives that day too." It isn't lost on Wendy that she felt unsafe her whole life and that Spirit proved to her that she isn't just loved and guided, but protected in the most profound way.

WHEN NOTHING IS FAMILIAR

Whether you're going to college or have lost your job, it can be a real struggle to grieve the loss of familiarity. Nothing is the same anymore, and that can cause you to feel powerless and scared. And when you're emotionally drowning from this feeling, Spirit says you might even go so far as to think, *Whose life is this, anyway?* I think about when I tore my ACL and was forced to wear sneakers onstage during my live events. Boy was I thrown by a lack of familiarity! I realize that on the surface, that may not sound as heavy as what you're going through, but what those shoes represented to me—a health crisis strongly connected to losing a familiar and comforting life with my ex-husband, Larry—created a deep sadness every time I slipped them on.

Mantra: I may feel lost and confused, but I'm resilient.

One of the most common ways that we lose a sense of familiarity is when we lose a cherished loved one to a passing—and one of the best ways that Spirit reassures us that it's okay to go on without that person is to make their souls known to the living in remarkable ways. After all, what's more familiar than receiving mind-blowing signs that remind you of a life you once shared with a person and soul you still love? This makes me think of a wonderful story about a woman named Allison, whose husband, Adam, died from a sudden, massive heart attack after playing tennis. Adam was only forty-seven years old at the time.

"When Adam died, my three sons, Andrew, Austin, and Addison, really wanted to be with peers who were also coping with the death of a loved one," she told me. "I felt a nagging belief that if I didn't model to them that the world is a safe, secure place and engage in it myself, then my boys would be challenged to do so. I needed to create a sense of security and familiarity for them, and other kids, in the face of the exact opposite."

To help families like hers regain their footing, Allison opened Adam's House, a facility that offers grief education and peer support to mourning children and their families in Shelton, Connecticut. There, families gather to draw support from their peers and gain new strategies for dealing with loss, whether it's the loss of a family member or friend. All programs are offered at no cost to families, as the foundation's goal is to help participants cope with their loss so that they may live their lives to the fullest.

Though Allison was deeply suffering from a lack of familiarity and safety at the time, a series of serendipitous events and validations from Adam's soul helped her to stay focused on her goal to open Adam's House. One of the most amazing signs occurred during a baseball game, which was emotionally hard for the family to attend since Adam had coached and adored the game himself.

"I was in awe of my son Addison's determination and commitment to honor his dad by still playing the game he loved," she said. At some point while watching the game, Allison reached into her bag to grab her camera to snap a shot of Addison at the pitcher's mound. "In my head, I heard the words, 'Take the picture,' so I did," she said. "And when Addie uploaded it to the computer, he screamed, 'Mom, whoa, this is NOT nothing!'" In the photo, you can clearly see a big, beautiful orb smack in the center of the picture. "I especially love that there's a blue heart over Addison," Allison said. "I can also see Adam's face just to the left of the heart."

Allison immediately forwarded the picture to her oldest son,

Andrew, who was away at college. The next day was his birthday, which was more than a coincidence. "I wrote, 'I know you miss Dad, but with tomorrow being your birthday, know he'll be there! This picture is a gift to all of us, but the timing tells me it's especially for you!'" At the time, Allison was still angry at God for her husband's passing, but the photo gave her the comfort and security of knowing Adam's soul was with her family. It also helped her trust that a bigger plan for Adam's House was unfolding.

Another reassuring sign from Adam's soul came after Allison found the perfect space for Adam's House, and the buyers requested a closing date of March 2—her late husband's birthday. "That made me feel a stamp of approval from Adam that we had chosen the right house and that the program would help a lot of people," she said. Then, during renovations, a student intern found a newspaper in the wall of the bathroom; it was the front page of an old copy of the *Philadelphia Inquirer* dated, you guessed it, March 2! Keep in mind, Adam's House is in Connecticut, not Pennsylvania—though the founder of a similar program, Olivia's House, and her son, who acted as mentors to Allison as she launched her program, were from the Keystone State. How's that for a serendipitous nod from above? "With every much-needed sign, message, and picture, we gained a lot of security and felt as if Adam's House was a safe and familiar space. We knew that powerful forces were at play."

Spiritual intervention didn't stop there. When the phone company came to Adam's House to hook up the TV and phone, a serviceman named Nestor fiddled with the boxes to determine which were obsolete and which were functional. When he got to the last box, Allison recalls Nestor saying, "This is your basic phone connection, so if you're going to call Addison, this is what you'll use."

Allison and Nestor were both immediately shocked by his words, as Nestor had never met Allison's son Addison, nor did he even know anyone else by that name. As Nestor said, "I don't even know an Addison. It's like someone put his name in my head and made me say it." Pretty incredible. In the face of all things unfamiliar, there's nothing more comforting than hearing from what was once a steady constant in your life.

TIPS FOR MENTAL AND SPIRITUAL GROUNDING

When a sense of safety and familiarity feels precarious or is lost, Spirit says to ground yourself in exactly what's missing—familiarity and safety. Visualization and self-talk will go a long way here. At the first inkling of a related negative emotion, Spirit suggests that you immediately say the words "stop, stop, stop" in your head and then replace that unsafe or unfamiliar thought with one that puts you at peace. For instance, you can close your eyes and visualize yourself inside a home or on a beach, with angels or near a loved one who's still in this world. You can also look in the mirror and reassuringly affirm your identity as a wife, mother, friend, and so on.

I was separated from Larry at the same time that I was dealing with perimenopause (talk about a one-two punch!) and constantly felt like a person whom I didn't recognize. I didn't know what was going to happen to me, and I felt unsafe and out of control. I had to learn to become independent and be solely responsible for myself, which is scary. To love and honor myself in a way that grounded me in the now, I'd look in the mirror and remind myself of who I was and what I meant to other people even when I, my world, and my wacky hormones were fuzzy to me.

This practice really worked when I tore my ACL too. Being so far from home at the time, I felt tremendously unsafe and in unfamiliar territory. Before I became a practicing medium, I had suffered from crippling anxiety. I didn't want to leave the house, which meant I rarely went shopping or to parties, and I liked staying home where I felt safe. But while I was in Hawaii, I was thrown out of my comfort zone, and then some. Here I was getting divorced, living on a tour bus, suffering a major injury twelve plane hours from home . . . and I didn't have anxiety because I had a tool to bring myself to a grounded mental place that worked for me.

Another idea is to look to figures of faith who bring you comfort. The Blessed Mother, Buddha, and Saint Thérèse of Lisieux, the patron saint of missionaries, florists, and the sick, are all comforting figures for me when I'm feeling turned around; but I suggest that if your loss feels especially burdensome, you go right to God as God is ultimately in control of everything. He can make you feel safe and in control faster than any other celestial being.

Finally, when dealing with issues specifically related to losing consistency and security, Spirit suggests a practice that establishes a recognizable routine in your life. You could, for instance, regularly imagine yourself filled with white light or surrounded in a bubble of white light during daily meditation or create a prayer ritual every morning to give you the sanctity that you desire. I also talk to God in the shower every morning, because it's a quiet time where my mind is at rest and I can address a higher power and listen to what He has to say to bring me back to my calmest self.

Good Mourning

Choose an activity that makes you feel unsafe because of an everyday loss or the passing of a loved one. This might be driving after a car accident or going out to eat by yourself after your spouse has died. In the name of creating a "new familiar," push yourself to take a baby step toward doing the activity on your own. If it's related to driving, start by slowly cruising down the street with your seatbelt fastened. If it's associated with eating out, simply order a cup of coffee at a local diner rather than a whole meal. With slow and steady progress, your goal will be a no-brainer in no time.

1

ON LOSING YOUR HOME

*L*eaving or losing a home, or a significant part of your home, can be a very difficult and emotional trial to endure. Whether the situation is in your control or beyond it, Spirit says you will grieve the experiences, people, pets, and feelings that you associated with that space. A home, after all, can act like a time capsule, a contained reflection on a beloved past.

There's a reason that the saying "home sweet home" has lasted as long as it has—if you're fond of your four walls, you're going to relish them and the memories they hold. Homes nurture and protect you in the most basic ways, but they also hold a special place in your soul when you make a house your home. So to no longer have a home that you once cherished so much can feel like an enormous loss. And when you lose your home sweet home, you also grieve your home's surroundings that gave it the character you miss—the neighbors, garden, location, and all the details that contributed to the life you built while living in that place and moment in time.

WHAT'S IN A HOME?

We lose homes for various reasons. You might make the choice to sell your home, or you might lose it to a natural disaster like a hurricane, fire, or flood. Your home could be forced from your possession due to a foreclosure, divorce, or death. Getting married, even though it's a joyful occasion, can cause you to leave one home for another, which can feel bittersweet. Grief around moving is even more amplified when you're leaving after experiencing another loss—say, because a loved one has died or you are separating from your spouse—since you have to process the first loss and then the loss of your home.

For so many of us, a home represents safety and stability. It can be a respite and a place where love flourishes. It's where you spend the core of your family time. A home is full of rooms where you can be yourself. At its very best, it's a beautiful, safe space—a place of memories where you've built your life and who you've become and are still becoming.

When I suffered from anxiety, I hated leaving my house, because my house was my safe place. My mom, however, always remind me that *I* was my safe place—not my home. She said that I had the ability to define what was safe and what wasn't, and if I held my safe place within me, then I could never lose it. No fire could burn it down, no financial crisis could force me to move. When your safe place is you, then you will forever feel at home.

SALVAGE WHAT YOU CAN, FOCUS ON THE FUTURE

When you lose a home, Spirit has the utmost compassion for this loss; however, they also emphasize that you should focus on as many positive outcomes as you can. If a natural disaster or fire took your home, concentrate on the fact that your life was spared. Be grateful for what you could salvage and don't focus on what you've lost. Consider the blessings and not the destruction. Perhaps you held on to your grandmother's china, parents' wedding album, or the blanket your great aunt made. Maybe your life was the only thing that was spared; Spirit says this should be enough. Your family can make new memories as long as you have each other.

I know a woman named Jen whose family's home caught on fire when Jen was just fourteen years old. Jen's family dog accidentally turned the dial on the stove to low when it tried to lick a microwave bacon tray cooling on the back burner; the house erupted in flames. Jen's family lost most of their home, and nearly all their belongings were ruined by heat, smoke, or water damage from the firefighters' hoses. The only items they saved were Christmas ornaments and family photos. Volunteers and contractors worked around the clock to get the family back into their home for the holidays. Community and church groups rallied to help, and neighbors took in the family of five during construction and donated their time, money, and belongings to make sure they had beds to sleep in and clothes to wear.

Even so, the fire took an emotional toll on Jen. "A house fire is traumatizing. It's the scariest thing I've ever experienced in my life," she said. Because Jen was the only person home at the time, she made the 911 call, could feel the flames' heat, remembers every smell and sound that came from the house ("crackles and shattering glass")—and to this day, she still suffers psychologically because of the event. More than twenty years later, Jen thinks of the tragedy every Labor Day. She says a prayer for every fire truck that races down the street, and she donates to families who have suffered the same loss.

Putting a positive spin on the event and focusing on what the family was able to salvage and gain has helped Jen cope. She looked to her mom for support at the time, who's since passed because of breast cancer. Jen described her as an "extremely positive, nurturing, and wise woman. She always explained to me that things could be replaced, but people can't." She also reassured Jen that since the house was thirty years old and needed a new roof, new appliances, and other updates they couldn't afford, it was a blessing in disguise because, she said, "insurance covered a lot of great improvements, including the kitchen of Mom's dreams and a new screened-in porch."

Mantra: I am my safe place, I am my home, I am my temple.

What's interesting is that during Jen's whole life before the event, she dreamed of what to do during a house fire, almost as if Spirit were preparing her for the trauma and subsequent loss. "I'd have nightmares as a child about my house catching fire," she said. "So I knew all the escape routes from the house and knew to grab photo albums placed in a cabinet next to the front door, just in case. I was prepared. When the fire happened, it was as though I had experienced it already and took all the necessary precautions when getting out of the house and then reporting it."

Jen wouldn't wish a house fire on her worst enemy, yet the universe gave her the tools she needed to pull through. Spirit says this was not a coincidence, but guided protection from the other side.

REFOCUS, REBUILD, AND REJOICE

Transitioning from one home to another is a great time to meditate on how you would like to rebuild both your life and your home. Even if you can't make the "perfect" move right away, you can ask Spirit to guide you to it. To do this, Spirit says to visualize during quiet meditations what you'd like your ultimate home to be like. As you do this, engage as many of your senses as you can. What does the layout look like? How does the home smell? What colors do you see? What music is playing in the background of a lazy Saturday morning? Would you like a sprawling deck with an antique porch swing or the infinity pool of your husband's dreams? Be specific, because Spirit honors the details. Co-create this project with them. Ask for clear and determined guidance from God, angels, loved ones on the other side, and other spiritual beings to place this home in your path—one that has all the comfort, safety, and stability of your old space plus the updated qualities you'd like in a new one. Consider the whole experience to be a chance to reinvent and start fresh.

No matter where you land, moving on from a home is a lesson in letting go. Hold on to memories, but don't play into any "should have been, would have been, could have been" thinking. Your life right now is what it is, and I believe that what doesn't kill you makes you stronger. That includes losing a home and being forced to rediscover what makes you feel surrounded by joy.

When your home is engulfed by a natural disaster, you have no choice but to let go of the space and the tangible memories it held. I know a woman named Amy who was forty-four years old when her childhood home was destroyed by the Tubbs Fire in October 2017 in Santa Rosa, California. "My parents were settling down for the night when they smelled smoke and saw the entire horizon ridge ablaze," Amy told me. "Tall trees on our property—oak, pine, fir—they all began falling. My mother grabbed a few items, and they drove toward Santa Rosa proper. The entire horizon to the north was burning. They fled with the clothes on their backs by chain-sawing, with the help of their neighbors, an evacuation path through a fallen tree." After a week of her parents not being able to gain access to their home, Amy learned through satellite technology that it was gone. "I had to call my parents to tell them the news," she said.

Amy grieved a tremendous loss, as that home had held a lot of meaning for her. "I was born and raised in that house," she said, "and it held cultural significance to me as a Japanese American and the hubbub of Japanese activity that always came from it, as my mother is a teacher of both Japanese dance and Japanese tea ceremony. There were annual events around the Japanese cultural calendar that made our home a gathering place for students, family, and friends, including the New Year, Girls' Day, and the opening of the winter hearth for tea ceremony. That home made me who I am today, and though I've lived around the globe, it is still how I self-identify."

Amy said she felt so attached because she remembers playing for hours outdoors amid the tree fairies, baking "mud pies," and riding her bike until dusk. "My home was the center of my heart and my parents' amazing parenting," she said. "It represented freedom and love and sent me into the world with security and self-assurance. My grief for the loss of that home is so deep."

Amy's family wasn't able to salvage anything more than a few pieces of jewelry—and all with heat damage. "We lost nearly everything—baby photos, Japanese artifacts, and family heirlooms.

I am half Japanese, and my parents' home is a testimony to my rich ethnic heritage." Amy said her home was like a "mini Japanese museum," filled with gorgeous antiques, hundreds of kimonos, custom-made wigs for Japanese dance, and beautiful tea utensils painstakingly brought over from Japan. Her father also lost his amateur photography collection, antique camera collection, a watch collection, and more. Amy's parents went back to the site repeatedly to search for her grandmother's diamond ring, but there was nothing to save under the mounds of ash and clay soil.

To honor where she grew up, Amy has celebrated the woods of Santa Rosa on her personal website, with quotations about the land and photos of her walking through similar woods around her home. "I made a 'home' for myself online when my original childhood home no longer existed," she commented.

For more than a year after the fire, Amy could barely discuss the event without bursting into tears and experiencing nightmares. She also suffered from a painful frozen shoulder, which can be associated with extreme stress, that grew worse as her nightmares picked up speed. In her dreams, Amy would walk through her home so realistically—and then wake up with tears streaming down her face when she realized it was gone. She also dreamed she was trapped in the back of the house and unable to escape. When her dreams were less haunting, they featured souls who were meant to help her heal. "They'd feature my grandmother, who's alive at ninety-seven years old and sick with dementia, yet in my dreams, she'd appear healthy and help me reconstruct a memory, along with two of my deceased grandfathers," she said. "I believe these dreams were meant to help me embrace my home for a final time and say goodbye."

Despite her heartache, Amy is thankful for a lot and has grown from her tragic loss. "My parents barely made it out of the fire, so I'm overcome with gratitude that they're still alive," she said. "I also have less attachment to material life now. For the past two years, I've given away jewelry and clothes to friends and strangers. Things just don't have the same meaning for me."

Amy's parents are currently in the process of rebuilding their home on the same site, though progress is slow because of heavy rains, a shortage of workers, and various permit delays. Her father, who's overseeing the project, is also retired and dealing with his own grief. Even so, the family is doing their best to move through their loss with grace and strength. Sometimes, that's all you can do.

Good Mourning

To honor the home you've lost, create a photo album of loved ones once enjoying that space. Place it in a cabinet near your new home's door, like Jen's family did, so that it's always in a safe place and can be easily grabbed in an emergency. In your new space, Spirit also suggests filling a time capsule with meaningful items and memories written on pretty slips of paper and burying it in the yard to dig up later. This way, if you ever have to move from this new house, you'll have a snapshot in time to dig up.

10

ON LOSING YOUR JOB

*S*pirit says that far too many of us rely on our jobs to determine our pride and self-worth. So when we lose or change a job, or even transition from one career to another, grieving this loss can take its toll. Your identity might take a hit, and your social status might change. This loss happens in the real world, but it has the potential to take an emotional and spiritual toll on you too. You might no longer feel worthy if you were once the primary breadwinner and now you're up at the crack of dawn sending out résumés and wondering whether to join a networking group. You might blame God for taking so long to put an ideal position in your path.

Though I've never been laid off from a job, I have left jobs that I liked and remember the toll it took on my happiness to transition out of them. When I was a teenager, I worked in the processing department at our local community pool with my cousin Lisa. We'd sign people up for memberships, take their photos, and give them their membership cards. We had a lot of fun doing this together, summer after summer, so it was a tricky transition for me to go from this type of easy-breezy job to having a "real job" as an inventory controller for an oil company once I graduated from high school.

There, I had more serious responsibilities than I had had at the pool; I was in charge of the drivers, I checked their worksheets, I made sure they were correctly recording the amount of oil that was being delivered to the day's locations—that kind of thing. When I married Larry and had the kids, I left that job but ultimately went back to the company to work at night because I needed health insurance. That time, I worked in credit collections and customer service, dispatching servicepeople to customers' homes and making sure people had heat when they lost it. Eventually, I left this position too, so that I could spend more time with my family.

In between each job, I missed how important I felt as a bona fide professional. I missed the camaraderie of my co-workers and lunch breaks where we'd shoot the breeze over a meatball sub. It felt good to financially contribute to the family pot, and it bolstered my self-esteem. It was also great to get out of the house regularly. I liked helping people in their time of need too, which is actually the best part of my job now as a medium. In a lot of ways, you could say that I'm a customer service rep working for Spirit!

The point is, I know what it's like to leave beloved jobs and feel how that can change you. After each position, no matter how busy I would become, I felt a little lost for a while because being a professional or working mom or inventory controller or whatever title I held or gave myself was my normal and an integral part of my identity. I was proud of how much I could accomplish in a day and how many people I could help in the process. So transitioning out of those jobs and into whatever I did next was always a struggle for me. But I would stay focused on the positive—spending more time with the kids or having more time to myself—and try not to feel out of sorts in the new roles I took on.

MOVING ON

It's easy to lose hope or faith when you've lost a job. You might look to God for protection and feel He's let you down. To both regain your faith in a higher power and position yourself for your next best gig (why not kill a few birds, right?), I suggest you put some serious visualization, Law of Attraction style, into action here. The Law of Attraction is a universal law that says you will energetically attract into your life whatever you are focusing on. The belief goes that if you focus on negative stuff, you'll invite bad luck and poor opportunities into your world; but if you focus on positive thoughts, you'll call in limitless possibilities and discover meaningful joy.

Sounds good, right? Spirit says the key to finding a fulfilling job is not to focus on superficial qualities that you'd like your awesome new job to have but to focus on the values that will allow you to feel fulfilled in your new position. When I try to manifest what's in my heart and mind, I like to start by thanking God for all the blessings in my life, and then I ask for what I desire, not what I want. There's a difference here, believe it or not.

Spiritually speaking, my guides tell me that a *desire* is more of a feeling or a wish, but what you *want* is more me-focused and greedy. To our human ears, it may sound like Spirit is splitting hairs with semantics here, but the differences have to do with how the universe interprets those words too. And that's important, as Spirit puts your desires in motion. So in terms of a job, visualize yourself in a role that you desire that makes you feel valued, respected, happy, not overworked, financially supported with good vacation time and health benefits, empowered, and in tune with your co-workers. Do *not* focus on a selfish want, like working at a prestigious company for the sake of status and recognition, or homing in on a robust salary with the intention of buying a new luxury car to out-Jones your neighbor. See the difference? If your intentions are pure and good, you will align with a job that is also pure and good. If your needs are selfishly motivated, you'll attract a garbage job—or nothing at all.

My client Marie is now forty-five years old but lost her first job when she was twenty-eight. She was working at a fashion label as a stylist when her new boss laid off her entire department just days after she was hired. Though Marie was initially depressed about losing her position, and terrified about being financially unstable, she also saw this as an opportunity to refocus her career goals. Marie loved working in fashion, but she had studied advertising in college and saw the job loss as a chance to jump into the field of copywriting. Why not try something different? Thanks to a modest severance package, Marie was able to go back to school to take a few refresher courses, which helped her put together a strong portfolio and meet with the best headhunters. And while this led to various interviews, she didn't land her dream job. This is when Marie knew that she had to engage the universe and some serious Law of Attraction mojo.

Every night before bed, Marie closed her eyes and visualized herself in her new job. She saw herself dressed in a gorgeous business suit, walking to work, then entering her office where happy, friendly faces greeted her. She envisioned sitting down at her desk, cranking out award-winning ad copy, and presenting it to a room full of impressed clients. She saw a boss shaking her hand, congratulating her on a job well done, and then handing her a paycheck with a bonus for working so hard and doing so well. She imagined herself having lunch with colleagues whom she adored and even flirting with a handsome co-worker! Finally, she thought about taking a dazzling vacation with her friends, thanks to a healthy benefits package.

Marie practiced visualizing this narrative for three weeks and refused to get discouraged when interviews went bust and job opportunities proved disappointing. Finally, after a month of manifesting, Marie landed a position at a high-profile agency with all the qualities she had desired. She never lost faith and never lost sight of her goal—and the universe rewarded her handsomely!

WHEN YOU'RE ON THE REBOUND

Spirit wants you to know that there's value to what you do in your job but that this shouldn't define who you are as a person. Losing a job is simply one of the many life changes that potentially occur on this plane—sometimes not once or twice, but many times in a lifetime—and Spirit prefers that you find value within yourself to bolster your self-esteem. Be the best parent, the best friend, the best spouse or child that you can be—allow *those* traits to define you. You are so much more than a worker. In a job, you are replaceable, but as a person, you are one of a kind.

Sometimes losing a job can help remind you of who you truly are. My client Jill lost two valuable jobs back to back—her dream job, which she held for ten years at a prestigious magazine publisher, and another, which she worked for only eight months at a medical imprint. In both instances, she had complained to the HR department about the reporting structure with hopes to resolve the issues she faced, but she found that when she did that, she was dismissed from both positions.

"I felt really helpless and out of control, like a failure," Jill told me. "It didn't help that during the first job loss, I was also going through a divorce. The second occurred as I was buying a house. It was so stressful that I lost ten pounds. I hadn't been unemployed since I was thirteen years old and had always put everything I had into my career, so getting fired shook my view of who I was. For it to happen a second time made me question whether I was at fault rather than the toxic workplaces."

Jill's self-esteem took a major hit, and for a long time, she didn't know which way was up. "I'm a born rule-follower and type-A achiever so to feel like everything in life fell apart was tough," she said. "The second time, I worried that I would never find full-time work again. The rejection and loneliness of job hunting took a toll." Her pride, identity, and sense of security suffered; "it was humbling to say the least," she said.

Jill's extensive mourning process involved the five stages of grief: denial, anger, bargaining, depression, and acceptance— though not necessarily in that order. "I felt it all," she said. "The first time, my grief lasted close to a year. I hadn't realized how bad the environment I was in had been for me or how worthless it had made me feel, and I had to do freelance work to get positive feedback and focus on myself and other parts of my life to restore that lost confidence. To be honest, I was more stressed by the job loss than by my divorce, except for the fact that as a divorced mom, I have to support myself and my kids. That's scary."

Despite how little she had liked working at the jobs that laid her off, Jill grieved those losses especially hard because she was struggling with a simultaneous loss of identity. "I define myself largely by my work," she said. Jill also noted that her father had quit his job when she was young, and it threw her family into turmoil, so it never crossed her mind to quit her own terrible jobs, even when they were hurting her morale. "In my mind, quitting was the worst thing anyone could do, and filing for unemployment was shameful," she said. "I probably should have quit my job a long time before it eroded my confidence. I was good at it but unfulfilled."

Mantra: I live and I learn, and my job doesn't define me.

Jill tapped into various coping mechanisms to help her get by during this rough time. For one, she leaned on her therapist, who quickly diagnosed her with a stress disorder from her first job loss. Jill also began running again for exercise and got into hobbies like cooking, which helped. She turned to her mom and friends for support. She went on two trips and fell in love. Because of all these things, Jill began to enjoy life much more. She said that taking time for herself between full-time jobs felt like a necessary step in her healing and in reinventing her life at nearly forty years old. "This whole fiasco taught me to rely on myself and honed my strength and survival instincts," she said. "I also better realize the important things in life that aren't work."

In retrospect, Jill recognizes that her loss led to a surprising, positive outcome. "It helped me come to terms with perfectionism and realize that I deserve happiness," she said. "The path I was on was not getting me there." She finds life more joyful and meaningful now, with her freelance lifestyle and increased optimism about the future. "I'm still looking for full-time work, but I'm holding out for a job that I'm happy with," she said. "I value myself more and am stronger as a person knowing I survived this. I accept that those jobs were not failures, even the short-lived one—just experiences I can learn and grow from. I refuse to let myself be undervalued ever again, and while I may not be cut out for office work, I have a range of skills I can pursue." Best of all, Jill said that she's never felt more emotionally, spiritually, or mentally fulfilled. Isn't that inspiring? If you're between jobs, embracing your job loss as a lifestyle gain may help you too!

Good Mourning

If you're out of work or between gigs, Spirit says this is a great time to grab your journal and reflect on what you've learned from your recent post, how you've grown, and how you had likely *outgrown* that job. What positive experiences can you take from working in that role? How did it shape and affect you? Express gratitude for what a new move will bring into your life, and free yourself from any negativity that you've attached to it. No burdens or regrets!

11

ON LOSING
FINANCIAL STABILITY

*p*eople are funny about money, and it feels devastating to lose it. Your identity, sense of security, pride, and relationships all take a hit. You may feel embarrassed, like a failure, and even betrayed by banks, your boss, family members who gave bad advice, or the government. You can suffer shock, fear, regret, resentment, and anger. Personal relationships might deteriorate, your health might suffer, and you might find it hard to move on. Your ego is affected if you're forced to move from one lifestyle to another. Spirit says losing financial stability can even affect your soul, because it can change who you think you are and how you view yourself. You might doubt your self-worth if you were once a provider for your family and no longer can be, and you may resent your partner if they're responsible for the loss of finances. Suddenly, your entire world comes crashing down all because of some unfortunate arithmetic.

Spirit says, however, that you shouldn't internalize and grieve a financial loss as deeply as those on this plane say you should. If you still have your health, that is of primary importance, and Spirit says to count your blessings and what you do still have, even if solid finances aren't one of them. They encourage you to remember and embrace your faith and who you are as a person. Spirit also emphasizes the importance of living within your means. You don't have to do without because of a financial loss, but you do have to learn how to spend carefully. At the end of the day, Spirit emphasizes that money is not the root of happiness, and the upside of losing it may be an opportunity to reprioritize your choices, values, and decisions.

PROCESSING YOUR PENNIES

A sudden and unexpected loss of assets, and the emotions that follow, can be hard to process. You might lose money to expenses related to an illness, a recession, poor investments, or even fraud. I've seen clients cry over material goods, property, or money that they've lost in a will.

Money is important because you need it to live and you may work very hard for it, but it should never be the crux of your identity. What makes grieving the loss of finances so trying, I think, is that it ties into other things that truly do matter. Spirit says it's not just about losing the cold, hard cash but about how your financial loss works into your plans for retirement, college savings, housing opportunities, lifestyle, and expectations for the future. A loss of financial security gets in the way of how you always saw your life playing out. You have to reconsider vacations, college savings, dinners out with friends and family, and any money that you were hoping to put aside for an inheritance for your grandkids. The loss becomes about altering plans, hopes, and dreams. It's about feeling like you didn't pull through for you or your family, and that self-evaluation will affect the way you feel about a financial loss.

My client Allison's mom Edie became hooked on a phone scam after undergoing a mind-changing illness, and the family lost a significant amount of money as a result. A few years before, Edie had nearly died from diverticulitis, and although she was sharp as a tack before the condition and surgeries, Allison said that afterward, something changed. "You could tell in her eyes that she wasn't all there anymore," she said. With Edie in this new mental state, a group of scammers took advantage of her. "The main scammer somehow started calling my mom and told her she had won a multimillion dollar lottery. All she had to do was pay the taxes," Allison said.

The scammers asked for $500 to $1,000 and sent Allison's mom to a specific Western Union location in town to send the money out. Edie did as she was told, and then waited. Nothing. Then the games officially began. Week after week, the scammers asked for $500, $1,000, $1,500 and sent Edie to different Western Unions all around town so that she didn't draw suspicion. All the while, she was pulling the cash from her savings accounts. "My mom even told my dad to sign withdrawal slips until his savings were gone too," Allison said. "Then she was taking it from her salary. Then her life insurance policies. Then the scammers told her to go to cash advance places. Then she tried bank loans. This went on for a couple of years at least." At one point, Allison counted out the Western Union receipts for three months, and the total came to about $23,000. "I stopped counting at that point," she said. "It was just too upsetting."

Allison found out about the situation when she received a phone call from a Western Union loan officer who said her mom was hooked into a scam. "Mom went there for a bank loan," she said. "When the loan officer asked what it was for, my mom got squirrelly. The loan officer pushed, and my mom admitted what she was doing. The loan officer got my information from my mom and called me. I appreciated the call, and it was the beginning of trying to get her loose from the scammers' hold."

Allison talked to her mom and dad and explained what was happening. They said they believed her, but it started again as soon as Allison went back to her home in Chicago. "Every time I went to my parents' house, we had the same conversation. I even had their phone number changed, but Mom would call 'Marcia,' and it would start all over again," she said. "Dad really didn't understand what was going on, but he said he wouldn't let her do it anymore. I even took them to a lawyer, which was useless." The lawyer basically said it was Edie's money that was being spent, and she could do what she wanted with it. He asked her if she understood that it was a scam and made her promise not to do it again. Allison said he was incredibly patronizing, and she was at a loss for what she could do next. When Edie finally realized what she'd done, she was embarrassed, yet she continued to send the money until it was all gone.

Allison said that she and her mom fought every time they talked. "I would receive calls from neighbors about her calling them for rides to take her to Western Unions on the bad side of town. Or to pick her up from one," she said. "I told her how dangerous it was to carry a purse full of money to some sketchy place. At one point, Mom even totaled her car and sent the insurance money to the scammers. We had talked about not cashing the check until I came home, and how we could use it to buy a small car for her. This started another fight. I absolutely blamed my mom for her poor judgment and curious behavior. I had no idea how to help beyond what I was doing, but I still fought, blamed, and shamed."

Mantra: Live your life, but live within your means.

When all of her parents' money had been spent, Allison said her mom and dad seemed shocked but were also able to quickly forget and move on. However, Allison grieved this money because a large part of it was to be passed on to her as an inheritance when her parents died. "I grieved by being angry," she said. "I was angry at my parents, but I was mostly angry at the trolls who did this."

She took matters into her own hands at one point and tried to talk to the scammers to get them to stop. "I was home one time and 'Marcia' called," Allison told me. "My mother and I sound alike, and it was hard to tell the difference between us. I talked to 'Marcia,' and at first, she believed I was my mom. She was asking why the money hadn't come that my mom had promised to send. I said I was sick, yet she insisted that I send her money to get the lottery money. She said it was to pay the taxes on the winnings. When I pushed further, 'Marcia' said she would never lie to me and was very slick. She would badger me with why it needed to be done and how it needed to be done quickly so I could collect the winnings. This woman told me how much to send and where. She eventually figured out I wasn't Edie, and she was angry. I was angry. I let out a rant of obscenities that would make a sailor blush."

Allison's anger was ripe at the time, and she still carries it with her. "I don't know if I'll ever get over it. It's not like there were millions of dollars, but it sure would have helped them in retirement and me, later in life," she said. "I've been working part time since I moved down south to take care of my parents. It's impossible to make money to retire when you're part time. I'm forty-eight, and retirement feels right around the corner. I'm getting to the age where people won't want to hire me much longer. Not having that money as a cushion is extremely detrimental. With my low salary, my 401K is basically pointless. I feel like I've wasted peak earning years that should have been the most productive for me. My mom has since passed, but by the time my dad dies, I'll be fifty, at least—he's ninety-five years old now. Not the time to start over without a cushion. It's quite depressing."

Though Allison has had trouble coping with the loss, her parents grieved on and off. She said her father didn't really react to the situation, and she's not sure how her mom truly felt when it was all said and done. "It coincided with her illnesses, so I don't know what was due to what," Allison said. "I know she was depressed. I know she cried about it. But she was never very good about sharing her feelings, so I don't know how much it affected her. She used to quilt and was very good at it. She was very good at all needle crafts. I'm pretty sure she sold some of her quilts to send the money to the scammers. Eventually, she stopped doing all of her crafts. She would also get very anxious when we discussed it. She would shut down when we discussed anything."

Allison tried her best to clean up the messy situation. "I moved to my parents' house and took care of everything that I could," she said. "Getting them out of debt. Making deals with companies after explaining what happened. Getting the people to stop calling. (They were relentless. They would call and hang up if I answered. Then call again. Over and over, all day long. Eventually, they stopped.) My parents went back to being retirees without any cares."

But Allison is still dealing with her loss. "I've talked with a lady in California who read one of my rants on Facebook," she said. "She contacted me about making a public service announcement and using parts of this nightmare. She eventually wants to do a documentary/movie and use our story. I'd be happy to help so others can learn. I'd love to figure out how to do more." Allison would also like to help herself. "I'd like to go to counseling to rid myself of the rage, but I have terrible insurance, and I don't have time."

Spirit says that part of what's so difficult about Allison's financial loss is that it is compounded by so many other everyday losses at once. She's simultaneously dealing with a loss of control, safety, hopes and dreams, an argument, trust, and grieving past regrets. But to grieve without resolution will only build up inside her, much more so than it already has. Spirit says that Allison would benefit from learning how to process this enormous grief with a counselor who, at the very least, could guide her back to a healthy relationship with herself and her remaining parent.

HOW DO YOU DEAL?

Spirit suggests coping with a financial loss by trying your best to accept the current situation and determine what matters to you. You can even give this ordeal a positive spin by selling the things you don't need—clothing, shoes, tech equipment—and reaping the emotional benefits of the purge too.

During my divorce, I suddenly had to be careful with money because the process was so expensive. I decided to sell a lot of things that I no longer needed—shoes, clothes, purses, cameras, you name it. I felt good doing this because I had accumulated a lot of stuff, and it was high time to get rid of it. It was taking up physical space in my house and emotional space in my life. Removing clutter from my closet helped me remove it from my mind—isn't it funny how that happens? Somehow, after selling all these things that I didn't need anyone, I felt much happier and clearer about how I would proceed as a newly single and independent woman. I realized that I didn't need all that stuff to make me happy; I could make myself feel good simply by realizing a life and identity I wanted to live.

You should always grieve your financial setback in a way that's right for you, but Spirit says to keep a few points in mind. Change what you can to get your money situation back on solid footing, but do this while accepting that you can't go back to the way it was. Don't look back; only move forward, one foot in front of the other. Perhaps there's a way that you can see this financial loss as an opportunity. Learn from your mistakes and figure out how to handle money differently. Guard your identity with care. You might have once valued your self-worth on the basis of your job title and plans for the future, and now you find yourself living with your spouse's parents in their basement suite. That's okay. Seriously, it is. Accept what is happening and don't give up on yourself or your finances. Work hard to get out of trouble, while valuing what is still left.

Do what you can to be sure that you're supported in every way that you can be. Fight the instinct to isolate yourself from others. Seek emotional support from friends and family, especially those who've gone through similar setbacks. Talk about your feelings with people you trust. Take your power back by recognizing that your loss isn't shameful or a secret and know that you can succeed again. Remember that you've made it through past challenges, and you will make it through this one. Don't dwell on the past or think too much about the future; stay in the present, and work toward your new goals. Learn from this mess. There's a lesson in everything. Test out the joys of a simpler life without surrounding yourself with so much material stuff.

Above all, Spirit says to realize that God doesn't care when you lose money, and that should matter. He cares about how you react to the situation that's bringing you grief (in this case, the financial loss) and how you handle yourself as a result. Sitting at home and pouting with a bottle of wine is not going to make God feel sorry for you. God wants you to continue to take care of yourself—loving, honoring, and respecting yourself and those around you. He doesn't want your financial status to define you as a person, and you shouldn't want this for yourself either.

Good Mourning

It's time for a mega purge! I challenge you to sell items that no longer serve you, whether they're clothes, vacation homes, time shares, dishes, jewelry, fitness equipment, you name it. Then put the money aside for a rainy day; don't spend it on more stuff! You'll be shocked at how good it feels to clean out the mental clutter too. If you fight financial loss this way, it leads to financial gain!

12

ON LOSING YOUR
HOPES AND DREAMS

I'll admit, this was a hard chapter for me to write because I feel so blessed to have achieved all my hopes and dreams in one lifetime; frankly, I never thought I'd accomplish so much! It's been part ambition, part happy accident, and the rest has been guided by Spirit. I adore my career, I have the best family, and I've always felt loved and supported by the people who matter to me. I work hard to stay in good health. I travel, meet inspiring people, and can support myself and donate to charities I care about. And let's not forget, *hello*, that I also have a closet full of gorgeous shoes and blinged-out bags like you wouldn't believe. What more could a girl ask for?

My life wasn't always such smooth sailing, though. When I suffered from crushing anxiety, I put a lot of hopes and dreams on the back burner. One dashed goal that really upset me was that I could never bring myself to go on family vacations because I was afraid to leave my house; I didn't feel completely safe in the outside world. I also knew that if I had an anxiety attack in public, I couldn't use the same tools to calm myself down that I used at home (basically pacing in my bedroom). So when my grandparents, cousins, parents, aunts, and uncles would all go on cruises or to Atlantic City for the weekend, I couldn't handle it. When they'd leave without me, I'd be okay in the beginning because I was so petrified, but then I'd get depressed that I was missing out on this bonding time and allowing my fear to stop me from doing something I wanted to do.

I always spent summers with my grandparents and took vacations with family when I was young, but when I was around eighteen years old and started living on my own, I began hibernating when the rest of my family was out having a good time. I allowed my fear to squash my hopes for far too long. So just this past year, I went on my first family cruise to Bermuda with all my cousins—there were twenty-eight of us! Given that I used to miss out on these kinds of trips, I felt so proud of myself that I was able to go. But I'll admit, there was a moment when I thought, *Look at what I missed out on all these years.* I'll never let my anxiety get in the way of traveling with my loved ones again! We had too much fun!

WHEN HOPES AND DREAMS DISAPPEAR

Many situations can cause you to grieve the loss of your future hopes and dreams, such as the end of a relationship, a job or entrepreneurial opportunity that went south, or a talent that you feel you never groomed to its fullest potential. Families with disabled children grieve the notion that their little ones' conditions will hamper their future, learning, or functioning ability. As with any loss of an ideal, you're grieving what you've imagined should happen but won't—what goals you or someone else should accomplish but can't. So when hopes and dreams don't come to pass, your expectations can be destroyed, along with your positivity and faith. Spirit says, however, that even as you grieve the loss of an ideal that you imagined for yourself or someone else, you must stay focused on what you *can* control and how you can more realistically bring other, or related, dreams to life. They want you to try to stay as positive as you can, even when experiencing a loss.

This loss is particularly hard because you're dealing with a what-if situation, which leaves room for your imagination to go wild. *What if caring for my sick wife hadn't held me back from becoming a famous singer? What if I'd secured the loan that would have helped me open a thriving vineyard during retirement? What if I'd been more affectionate toward my spouse, which could have saved our marriage?* Losing something that hasn't happened leaves an opening to fantasize about what the outcome could have been, even if you have no proof that it would have turned out the way that you'd wished. You don't know what would have been, but the assumption, of course, is that it would've been better than where you are now—and that may not be the reality.

It's normal to grieve the loss of hopes and dreams, but Spirit says to keep your position on this loss in perspective. Seriously. It reminds me of when I channel a soul who tells a living loved one not to romanticize an ideal that could have brought about a different outcome, whether it's taking the person to a different doctor or not allowing a person to drive a car the night they died in a car accident, because the outcome of their what-if thought might not have changed their destiny. The outcome might feel possible, but its reality is only in your head.

STAY OPEN TO NEW GOALS

To cut down on what-ifs, and the feeling that you've botched your hopes and dreams forever, Sprit says to do as much as you can right now to dip your toe into the dream you feel you're missing out on. For instance, I always wanted to be a Dallas Cowboys cheerleader. Clearly, I'm not one nor will I ever be, but that didn't stop me from booking a tour of the stadium, buying boots and pom-poms at the gift shop, and getting photos and autographs from all the cheerleaders I admire! Rather than allow the what-if to take over my soul, I came as close to having the dream, or a version of the dream, as I could. And you know what? It was extremely satisfying!

Spirit says that the major reason we get so upset over feeling we've lost out on hopes and dreams is that we worry that we haven't fulfilled our purpose. But Spirit says that when it comes to your life's purpose, if you are meant to achieve a goal in some way, shape, or form, God will present opportunities that keep bringing you back to it. Those opportunities might be creative twists on what you imagine, but they are situations that will fulfill you regardless.

For example, perhaps you're a talented singer. Your purpose might not be to become a famous opera singer or the winning contestant on *The Voice* but instead to share your talent during open mic nights in town and with the church choir. Maybe singing in a popular wedding band and bringing happiness to other people on their big day is your true purpose. This might be because other priorities such as caring for a sick parent or raising children are meant to take top billing here. In this kind of situation, then, you don't need to grieve unfulfilled hopes and dreams but recognize that they're simply a variation on a theme and that you have every reason instead to celebrate your gift—just in a different way. You must realize that God's intentions may not align with your worldly dreams and trust that He knows best. With God and your soul's journey, flowing along with the universe's plan holds more weight than selling out concerts around the country.

The topic of squashed hopes and dreams often comes up when a couple has trouble growing their family. But again, God's and the soul's intentions may be different from yours. I know a husband and wife who haven't been able to make a baby. At the start of their journey, the husband wasn't sure that he wanted to have kids at all, as he didn't come from a very nurturing home. The couple underwent many rounds of in vitro fertilization that didn't take, and while this might have been enough to break a relationship, it actually made theirs more solid. Spirit says that strengthening their bond through this painful situation was more important than producing a child. The husband came to value the importance of family and unconditional love, and his soul really grew.

Another woman I know named Jessica and her husband, Josh, have faced similar trials and have had to constantly readjust their expectations—let's just say their backup plans have had backup plans. During their journey to grow their family over the past five years, Jessica had two ectopic pregnancies, which resulted in the loss of her fallopian tubes. She then moved on to in vitro fertilization, and after three challenging rounds, she lost three babies at six weeks. Now the couple is trying surrogacy, and if that doesn't work out, they will try adoption; but so much change has caused Jessica to feel discouraged and like her dreams will never be fulfilled. "Given all our obstacles so far, becoming a parent feels very far away," she said. "There was never a time in my life when I didn't see myself as a mother. I've wanted this since I was a little girl. Those hopes and dreams crumble more and more with each passing day."

Needless to say, experiencing disappointment and then having to readjust to a new baby-making plan has taken its toll on Jessica. She said that seeing babies or pregnant women out in the world, attending other women's showers, passing the adorable baby department in a store, watching movies and TV shows that feature happy new moms, and honoring the anniversaries of her children's losses are all triggers that bring her way down. "I never know when an emotional outburst will happen," she said. Jessica has experienced severe anxiety, panic attacks, depression, and mood changes because of her challenging parenting journey. "I'm not the same person I was before—sometime around the third loss, I began to change," she said. "It took me a few years before I could admit that I needed help." To have her hopes and dreams redefined over and over has been "dizzying, and in many ways, absolutely soul crushing," Jessica told me. "It's a feeling I never thought I'd have to endure. There are some hopes and dreams in this world that are easier to get over, like not being able to afford a vacation to a place you'd always wanted to go or not being in the career you've always wanted to be in. They're not as upsetting because you can still control those dreams. You can save money or quit your job and start over. But having hopes and dreams of seeing yourself and your spouse in the eyes of your children and then having that ripped away from you—it's uncontrollable and unfathomably painful."

Having to constantly experience loss, and then readjust her hopes, only to then have those hopes denied, has made Jessica feel she's not living her purpose. And as I mentioned earlier, the what-ifs here are hardest for her to deal with. "I think about the five kids we've lost all the time," she said. "I wonder what they'd look like, what their personality would be like, what they'd have been when they grew up, and would they be happy."

Jessica and Josh realize that having a family isn't a guarantee, and Jessica admits there's a lesson here. "It's been tough to swallow, but we've learned that moments in your life won't always go how you want them to no matter how much you try or pray," she said. Though Jessica and Josh are still hopeful for a child through surrogacy, they're finding other ways to "parent" a little one in need. "We rescued a puppy recently that's filled up a little bit of the hole in our hearts," she said. "He has made our lives so much better and brighter." Clearly, their pup is no substitute for a child, but as they move to the next leg of their journey, it's a variation on a parenting dream that seems to do the trick.

Mantra: Live to dream, and dream to live.

As I listened to Jessica and Josh's story, Spirit assured me that this couple would be parents, but that right now, learning how to love, respect, and support each other in new ways is the priority. Sometimes when a couple faces infertility challenges, anger, bitterness, and blame come spewing to the forefront of the relationship, yet with Jessica and Josh, there is an increasing intention for affection, compassion, and understanding. I also felt that their children's departed souls were actively placing opportunities in the couple's path to have a family and that the surrogacy route is as much about their own story as the surrogate's. The surrogate's journey is to help another family have a child, and her growth is intimately tied into this couple's growth. Their story is so much bigger than the two of them producing a child; again, it's about expanding their love, as they try for a family, and intertwining their journey with the surrogate's journey. Theirs is a perfect example of how God's plan for our hopes and dreams can be much more involved than we could ever envision for ourselves; we simply have to do our best to trust and watch it unfold.

Good Mourning

Before you get out of bed tomorrow morning, take a few minutes to think about a hope or dream that's been deferred or that you fear you'll never reach at all. Then spend time that day either planning a goal that helps you reach that dream or a variation on the dream. Do you wish you were a famous playwright? Outline the first act of a play and consider what it would feel like to produce it at a local playhouse. Do you feel you missed out on your childhood dream of becoming an engineer? Call your local library and organize a community Maker Faire for kids. Spirit says you'll be pleasantly surprised by opening your mind and flexing your creative muscles like this!

13

ON LOSING YOUR YOUTH

*L*et's be honest: getting older can be horrible. Horrible! But it doesn't have to be, and it's not just a vanity thing. When I mention losing your youth, you might think about grieving smooth skin and gaining weight, but it's so much more than that. It's feeling like you can't get up after a night out or you can't crawl out of bed without too many aches and pains. It's about not being able to eat or exercise like you used to. I remember being able to lose five pounds in three days by eating just hot dogs, cottage cheese, and crackers. Now, it takes me three weeks to take off half that! I mean, if I even look at a hot dog the wrong way, I'll put on five pounds.

Grieving your youth also involves realizing that just because your mind wants to do something doesn't mean that your body's capable of it. You're marching closer to death, and that has a big impact in your life whether you fear it for yourself or for loved ones. The whole ordeal can be frustrating, annoying, and sad, to say the least. It's as if your body changes overnight while the rest of you is peacefully asleep. Unless, of course, insomnia is part of your aging process. The changes never seem to end!

This past year was the first time I noticed that my body was aging in a way that really affected me. During my divorce, I put all of my energy into exercising, eating right—and then I hurt my knee. Suddenly, I couldn't do as much to help myself, and my body seemed to take advantage of this setback to age like crazy. Remember, I'm also in perimenopause, so it's a wonderful double whammy. I've noticed that my knees are wrinkling now, the skin on my face is losing its firmness, and there's a little spare tire around my midsection where my trim stomach used to be. And no matter how much I try to help myself, nothing's working to change what's changing. Every day, I have to remind myself of the fact that I'm fifty-two years old and that my body simply looks and functions differently. I tell myself that I need to accept my new life and body. If I don't, I'll push myself too hard—and right into bed with an injury!

When I make it a point to be aware of what's happening to me as I get older, then I can make adjustments and changes that help me out. For instance, I now let myself sleep in and don't book appointments at 8 a.m.; I might make them for after lunch instead. This gives me more energy during the day. I also work out later in the morning than I once did, so that I can lounge in bed and have more oomph for my exercise routine. I space out my agenda so life feels less hectic too. That kind of thing. Basically, I try to be mindful about what needs to get done within my new reality. Hey, just because I'm slowing down doesn't mean I'm going down!

SPIRIT ON AGING: MEH

Spirit has compassion for the aging process but doesn't make too big a deal about it. As with many everyday losses, they point out the positive side of what you perceive to be your negative situation. Have you noticed that each time you feel you've lost something,

Spirit is right there to tell you what you've gained? So maybe you can't drive yourself to the store, but isn't it nice having an Uber pull up to the door so that you don't have to fight for a parking spot in a crowded lot? Or perhaps you can't go out like you used to, but isn't this now a great chance to rediscover your love for playing cards, crocheting, or painting? You don't need a job to define you as you age, and without your old physical hobbies, you have more time to hang out with loved ones on the sofa. Reflect on your life and pass on stories and lessons to a younger generation. Spirit says to use your free time wisely and teach others the wisdom you've gathered through the years.

I always find it touching to watch friendships blossom in retirement homes, where the elderly share their life's tales with each other and with younger family members who are eager to visit and listen. My client Kristina's Nana made a close friend named Matilda while Nana was living in a nursing home. Every week Kristina visited her Nana and Matilda and brought them all kinds of treats—handmade jewelry, homemade cookies, and their favorite, a fried chicken picnic. The two women loved sharing stories from their very different upbringings—Nana's as an Italian immigrant from New Jersey and Matilda's as an African American from North Carolina. They'd tell them to Kristina and frankly anyone who'd listen.

Kristina kept up these weekly visits for years, and sometimes brought her friends along. After Kristina's Nana died, Kristina's family started inviting Matilda to holiday meals. Kristina welcomed her into their home with open arms and valued their sweet friendship, regardless of the age gap. Their bond picked up where Matilda's relationship with her Nana had left off.

Part of why Spirit isn't too attached to the topic of aging is because there is no aging process in Heaven. Aging is related to our human bodies and not our souls. And when Spirit talks about growth, they refer only to soul growth. Now, if a child dies young, that soul might show itself to me as an older child if its parents dream or think about the child being that age. It might even show itself with defining characteristics like blue eyes or curly hair, but again, this is based on how someone imagines the soul to be growing in Heaven. Parents want to know what their children look like on the other side, and Spirit will show me a soul that has grown in this way. Parents will always then say that's how they envisioned their child, which is a validation that the soul has in fact matured and is aware of their parents' wishes.

So Spirit shows us growth in a visual language because that's how we understand and interpret it here; I don't believe the soul literally ages in Heaven. In fact, showing a loved one that a soul has grown is intended to bring comfort and help the person being read to understand that the soul is advancing through higher levels, or stages of soul maturation, from learning various lessons on the other side. As an interesting side note, I've also seen souls come through as *younger* than when they passed, like when a mother loses her teenage child to a drug overdose but fondly remembers that child at the age of six. This doesn't mean the soul has regressed, but that the image is meant to validate the parent's thoughts and offer them comfort.

I've also channeled plenty of souls who have spiritually matured well beyond what the average soul achieves after passing. If a child dies at birth, Spirit will make me feel like I'm holding a baby in my arms that is growing and growing. A few times, this imaginary baby has grown a lot more than other souls! I might feel like the child zooms from being a very small infant to a very tall thirty-something, and that tells me that the child has been grow-ing by leaps and bounds on the other side. I might then see details that align with a parent's perception of what the child now looks like—for instance a full head of hair, a mustache, a strapping build, eyes like his father's. This speaks to my earlier point that the details I sense are meant to bring comfort to the parent I'm reading.

Another sign of enormous soul maturity is if a child dies young and I see their body at this age but am made to feel like the soul inside the child is much older. I once channeled a little girl who was four when she passed but felt like she was forty years old at the same time. This was a very old, wise soul; Spirit was making me feel that she was spiritually mature beyond her years.

SPOOKED ON AGING

One of the major reasons that we grieve the aging process is that we are afraid. Maybe you're afraid of dying, of being too reliant on others, or of not looking or acting like the person you've known your whole life. Maybe you're afraid of becoming a burden to your family, or even to well-meaning strangers. But you shouldn't fear these things, Spirit says. You can cross the street and get hit by a car and die tomorrow. Age isn't the only factor that affects how you move through life and how your identity changes.

I can't tell you the number of souls that I channel who tell me that it was the *quality* of their years that mattered versus the *quantity* of them. Unexpected illnesses and freak accidents all took their lives when they weren't expecting it, and aging had nothing to do with their fate. After all, Spirit repeatedly says that when it's your time to pass, it's your time to pass. We are all given a win-dow of time in which our bodies will die, and specifically when we pass during that window is up to various factors, including our choices, our lessons, and lessons that are meant to be learned by those around us. When you think about the unknown that's ahead of you in these terms, you realize that you can't control the future and might as well surrender to whatever God has in store for you. At least that's what I do.

Mantra: I might be an oldie, but I'm still a goodie.

Some people who mourn their age are mostly concerned about visual changes and the impression that this leaves on others. I know a woman named Loren who's forty-eight years old and began to grieve the loss of her youth when her hair began falling out in clumps over a nine-month period. "Nobody could really figure out what was going on," she said. "The doctors said it was either stress-related or age-related alopecia. Great." Since then, Loren's had trouble looking at herself in the mirror and embracing how her body's evolving. "I despise the mirror, because it shows me how I'm not young anymore. Every day there's a new wrinkle, a new blemish, and dark circles under my eyes. I don't like watching television because everyone looks so perfect and young. It just depresses me. My breasts sag and my legs don't look the same." She said that not only does she fib about her age all the time, even on Facebook, but she lies about her children's ages too! "I lower their ages by a year or two," she said. "I'm offended if people ask me about my age and get easily agitated over this. I do not want anyone to know!" When she thinks about it, Loren suspects her hang-ups are as much aesthetic as they are related to grieving past regrets. "I dream and daydream about being younger and getting to do my life over. I see my beautiful young daughter and feel pangs of jealousy. She has her whole life ahead of her."

Spirit says many of us are afraid of the external factors that change as we get older, which contributes to our overall fear of aging and the losses we grieve along with those factors. You may lose your career, leave your house and move into a nursing home, adjust your lifestyle, and tighten your finances. Your kids will grow up and move away, and little by little, your friends will pass on. Your memory may start to change, and you may not be able to communicate the way that you once did. You will no longer be as active as you used to be.

Age-related milestones can remind us of time passing—with good times behind us and frightening ones ahead—which contributes to our grief too. My client Tess, who's seventy-one years old, said that she's actively mourned her age at three key junctures in her life. The first was when she was no longer young and hip, a time in which she also described herself as a knockout. "I was tall, lean, and had dark hair and eyes. I embraced the 1970s and the 'British invasion' head-on with Beatles music, straight hair, and miniskirts," she told me. "I was a flirt and enjoyed it when men flirted with me. I was witty, sarcastic, and charming. I dated my share of bad boys until I met and married a good man and moved from the city to a small town in Virginia. And had children. That was when I saw my youth, vitality, and body image beginning to deteriorate for the first time." At that point, Tess said that no matter how much she dieted or worked out, she wasn't the same woman she had been twenty years before.

In her late forties, Tess experienced her second reality check when she temporarily separated from her husband, and she and three of her single girlfriends took a Mediterranean cruise. "Tall, dark, and handsome Greek men were in every port!" she said. "Yet they were dancing, dining, and drinking with women half their age. That's when I realized that women my age were invisible to eligible men my age—another reason to mourn the fact that I was getting old. I was losing my youth, self-assuredness, and optimism at breakneck speed. I mourned the loss of my youth a second time and coped by going back to the safety net of my husband."

Tess's third and most poignant benchmark came when her best friend, Pat, whom she describes as "a blend of Mother Earth and Mother Teresa," died of a massive heart attack while Tess was talking to her on the phone. "I was rudely reminded that death comes to steal away the finest," Tess said. "She was a devout Catholic and the epitome of what Proverbs 12:4 calls 'a virtuous woman.' I know that's why she said she saw an angel in white hovering over her as she lay dying. Certainly, she was being gently lifted to Heaven." This is when Tess said that she saw her mortality staring her in the face. Even so, she's not afraid to die. "I am a woman of faith and expect to see Pat and my other loved ones who have gone before me on the other side. I'm more afraid of becoming ill or incapacitated and being a burden on my family than I am of leaving this plane." This last concern is very common among those of us who feel our age.

DON'T FEAR THE UNKNOWN

Spirit says that what most of us are ultimately afraid of when we age is the unknown. Yet Spirit says not to worry. God doesn't want you to curl up in a ball and wait to die. You must get out there and remember that your whole life is about growing and experiencing.

Sure, you're getting older, but you're leaving behind a legacy too. Make that your focus, and make sure it counts.

My friend Shelley is sixty-eight years old, and she often bemoans the fact that her body is showing its age. Even so, she's determined to live each moment with gusto like it's her last. "Where do I begin?" she asked me. "I wake up each day with tight muscles even when I haven't done any exercise. My neck has been a sore spot of late. It's difficult to bend down and get off the floor after being physically active for well over forty years. I've always been a runner, aerobic dancing instructor, cycling instructor, Pilates teacher, barre teacher, hiker, outdoor biker—you name it. I once could leap out of bed and exercise seven days a week! Not anymore."

Shelley added that her vision is also deteriorating, and she relies on night vision glasses and reading glasses though she once had perfect vision and never had to wear contacts or glasses. Shelley also said that when she looks in the mirror, she misses the loss of fullness in her face and wants to scream at the loose, sagging skin on her upper arms. "I used to be told I had great arms," she said. "The loss of elasticity and the thinning of the skin is not something I'm proud of!"

In retirement, Shelley can travel all she wants, but with decreased muscle mass, she worries about being "unable to hoist my own suitcase in the overhead bins and relying on someone to drive. Being independent for years to come is my greatest wish." And while she doesn't fear death for herself, Shelley does fear it for her loved ones. "As I age, they age as well, and it's the fear of being a *survivor* without their love and affection that scares me most," she said.

Shelley is obviously aware that her body is changing and showing its age, and while she cannot control this, she realizes that she can control how she reacts to this inevitable process. Spirit finds

Shelley's grieving rituals refreshing, as she grieves her loss not by crying in her smoothie, but by fighting the changes in her body. "I actively mourn by continually moving, continuing to ride my bike, and walking everywhere I can. I do barre class and Pilates. I'm always the oldest gal in any class. My body is doing what it's doing, but I don't have to accept every last detail of it. I strive to stay as young and healthy as I can."

Spirit says that a final option, acceptance, is to give in to the aging process and move through it with grace and wisdom. Welcome what aging brings into your life—wisdom, inner strength, and the like. You don't need to control or fight a normal process that happens in your body. You can let your hair go gray and laugh lines form deep grooves in your face, and both will show a life well-lived. Aging can be a beautiful process if you take on a healthy perspective about it.

Good Mourning

Aging doesn't need to be an albatross around your wrinkly neck! Take an elderly relative or friend to lunch and ask them what they appreciate about the aging process. Notice when they smile about craft class and can't stop gushing about their new friend down the hall at their retirement home. Your joys will be simpler as you age, but they'll also be richer and full of insight. Grieve, but then move on to a more positive perspective gleaned from real-world truths like the ones you'll hear that day.

14

ON LOSING YOUR "FULL NEST"

When your kids fly the coop, leaving an "empty nest" behind, you might grieve a number of losses at once. You might feel like you've lost your sense of purpose and wonder what you're supposed to do now that your kids are moving on with their own lives. You might struggle with wondering whether they will still care about you and how to fill the void that's left after they're gone. You might question whether you did a good job raising them and whether you've sent them down the right life path.

Let's face it: as a parent, you're used to being in control of everything, including your kids' lives, but once your nest is empty, you can't control where your kids are, who they're with, what they're eating, how they're driving, and, and, and. Spirit says that empty nest syndrome can be the starting point of relaunching your life with an exciting new identity, or it can send you into an emotional downward spiral if you're not careful. Which path would you rather be on?

WHEN BIRDS OF A FEATHER
DON'T FLOCK TOGETHER

Empty nest syndrome, as it's typically called, occurs when parents feel sad, lonely, and filled with grief when their kids leave home. Spirit says it's normal for you to want your kids to grow up to lead independent lives but then feel a humungous sense of loss when they do. They might head off to college, have their own relationships, and/or start their careers. Some describe their leaving as bittersweet, because on one hand, you've raised your children to be independent enough to live without you, but on the other, well, living without them can be hard to swallow. Grief, depression, a loss of purpose, loneliness, loss of connection, and sadness can easily set in.

Clearly, parents grieve this process because the center of their world is gone. You still love your partner, but your relationship changes and you go from intense parenting to making suggestions from afar, if that. Although you've raised your kids to be capable of making it on their own, you can't help but wonder whether their separation means that they don't need you anymore. You've shown your kids how to be independent, but now you're forced to be more independent too. All of your best intentions and efforts feel like they're coming back to bite you in the tush!

Until you comfortably readjust and settle into new roles, empty nest syndrome can lead to the loss of your identity. If you've always seen yourself as coach dad or PTA mom, you may question your new role and purpose. Realize that it's going to take time to reinvent yourself. Who are you now, if you're not a full-time parent? As your identity as a parent changes, you may feel more like a friend, casual confidant, or walking ATM. Old age might even feel more present than ever, with thoughts about mortality coming out of nowhere.

I know a dad named Brian who had a really hard time when his son Greg went to college. Until then, Brian considered himself a stay-at-home dad above all else and wore that title as a badge of pride. He cooked for his family, organized his son's extracurricular sports activities, was the chauffeur when Greg or his friends needed a ride anywhere, and made a point of being front and center in Greg's life. His wife worked full time and celebrated her husband for all he did. So when Greg was no longer around, Brian went through a major identity crisis. Without Greg to care for, he felt like half of himself was gone. Brian found a part-time job at Home Depot, which helped occupy his time and helped him gain a new identity as a professional. He also volunteered with an inner-city organization that took kids to events, games, and activities that they might not have access to on their own. And while this didn't fill the hole that Greg's leaving had left behind, Brian gradually reclaimed his life to a satisfying degree. He was able to embrace a new and more mature relationship with his son and with himself—not despite Greg's absence but because of it. He wasn't a dad who butted into his kid's life but supported it.

Personally, I didn't suffer from an empty nest because when my son, Larry, went to college, my grandmother was sick and I was just beginning to film *Long Island Medium*, so I had distractions that made my life very busy and took me on a different path—simple antidotes to getting over empty nest syndrome. However, I can imagine what it feels like because when I'm alone in the house, have time to myself, and the kids are gone, I do miss having them around. I text them a lot, but I always reflect at the same time on how thankful I am that they're good kids. They support themselves, and they're safe. Though my nest is empty, this is what I've always wanted for my children. When I think about all the fun times I used to have shopping with Victoria and sitting at baseball games watching Larry play as a kid, my heart sinks. But then I get over it and just run around the house naked to celebrate my freedom!

Everyone has these moments of missing their family as it once existed and grieving those changes, but I try not to let myself get caught up in them. If I have down time in which I'm thinking about my empty nest, my mind also goes to my parents, and I call them to find out how they're doing. If I'm missing my kids, they're probably missing me too. Especially since they're older.

My mom dealt with her empty nest differently. She said that it was difficult for her when my youngest brother, Michael, left home at age eighteen, since he didn't move next door like I did at age twenty-two. With my brother, Mom said it was especially tough because there were no cell phones back then, and they primarily communicated through letters—some up to ten pages long! And although I moved to the house next door when I got married and finally moved out, Mom said she still felt my absence because we were such close friends and did a lot together. Mom said she was happy for me, but it wasn't the same as having me around all the time.

After my brother and I left home, Mom said her relationship with us changed, but in a healthy way. She gave us space to live our lives and encouraged us to make our own choices, for better or worse. Eventually, Mom came to appreciate the advantages of an empty nest. "Sleeping with the bedroom door open was nice," she laughed. "I also got to spend more time with my husband. It freed me up to get involved with scrapbooking, which let me reminisce on childhood memories. I started journaling and spent more time with adult friends, talking about what we were doing with our time and not just what the kids were always up to." Mom said that what made an empty nest easiest on her was making sure that I and my brother knew that we could always come home when we wanted to.

READJUST, AND TAKE FLIGHT

To help you adjust to your empty nest, Spirit points to a few things you can do. Rather than feel down, try to reframe this time as one of relief and pride that your kids have the wherewithal to march forward with their lives—similar to how my mom did. It's normal to feel anxious about what to do with your time, so book yourself silly. Think about how you'll take care of yourself now that you aren't taking as much care of others. Self-care and reaching out for additional social support outside the family, even with a counselor if you need it, can help with this. Dig into hobbies, your career, new friendships, and traveling. Connect with others who are going through the same thing as you. Work on yourself, strengthen your marriage, and play outside your comfort zone. Create new routines like morning walks or evening hikes with your pets and family. Turn empty rooms into special places—meditation or crafting spaces. With extra square footage on your hands, you might even move into a different place. But expect to experience the loss of a home if you do decide to downsize. This could actually make an empty nest harder to deal with. But it's all normal and all okay.

What you don't want is to hound your children with endless emails, calls, and text messages, which can cause guilt and anxiety. Keep calls and texts to a reasonable number. Be sane, people! Follow your children's lead. Again, realize that your role is changing, and honor that commendable shift. Your children may need you in a different way, and you may need to show them the same.

I'm especially proud of how my client Renee handled her empty nest syndrome. She has two daughters who've successfully left home; both have graduated from prestigious colleges and are thriving in the world. "The nest was totally empty when I turned fifty-three," she told me. The transition wasn't easy, however. Renee's first child chose to attend a challenging college, so her loss was put on the back burner as she worried over her eldest's emotional well-being. "I missed her but found that my worry outweighed my loss," Renee said. "She also played lacrosse, so I had many opportunities to visit without looking like a helicopter parent." When Renee's second daughter left for college a seven-hour drive from home, she worried for other reasons. What if she got sick, sad, or needed a home-cooked meal? She was states away!

"Overall, I mostly felt sadness, anxiety, and loneliness," Renee said. "The feelings presented themselves as me becoming a social media stalker and overtexting. Not knowing where the kids were, who they were surrounding themselves with, whether they were eating healthy food, and whether they were sleeping made me worry a ton!" Renee said she's still guilty of overtexting, but her kids know they don't need to respond right away. "The oldest rarely had time to call during college but now calls my husband on the way to work and me on the way home," she said. "My youngest is very good about calling. I also visit and take their friends out to dinner, which makes everyone happy."

And although the family makes the new arrangements work, Renee said she also feels a loss of control over their daily lives. "I did a lot of thinking and hoping that all my talks about being a good person, persevering, enjoying life, and finding joy stuck. I miss seeing them in their beds and hearing their thoughts," she said. "Peeking around the corner and seeing them on their computers was really comforting. I always knew they were safe."

Renee said her relationships with her kids have changed, but thankfully, not in an upsetting way. "I think both of my girls appreciate me more now than when they lived with me, and they enjoy my company more," she said. Even so, Renee still grieves the shift in her role as a mom. "I went from being a full-time mom to being a mom-on-call. And I take that call whenever it comes. I have a separate ringer for my girls and am there for them at all times," she said.

Mantra: My house is empty, but my heart is full.

To cope with her loss, Renee thinks about how proud she is of the adults her kids have grown into and tries to spend more time with her own friends playing mahjong. She reads more articles for work and has more meaningful conversations with her husband than in the past. Even so, Renee said that life still doesn't feel "normal." "Especially when I miss my children, I need to force myself to remember that I raised them to be strong and follow their dreams," she said. "They are doing exactly what I hoped for even though I miss them tons."

If after readjusting your expectations, self-perception, and activity agenda, you're still not feeling better, Spirit says to lean on souls in Heaven that get it, such as your departed grandparents, who went through this decades before. In prayer, ask them for support during this time. Visualize what it was like for them when your parents first left home, and how they must have felt. By imagining them in your mind's eye, you're calling upon their energy for support. In fact, Spirit says their souls are with you at the exact time that you are thinking of them in this way.

Good Mourning

Did your child leave behind an empty or unused room that's causing your empty nest syndrome to feel more pronounced? Use it to bring you joy instead of heartache! Turn it into a den, an exercise room, a game room, or a crafting space. Choose an activity that you put aside while raising the kids and devote yourself to it in that room. Use your free time to take care of *you!*

15

ON LOSING YOUR ROUTINE AFTER RETIREMENT

Spirit says the hardest part about retiring is losing your routine, which includes redefining all the details that go into having a full and satisfying day. You might feel bored and struggle to figure out what you're going to do with your time and who you'll spend it with. I've even noticed that some of my clients' health deteriorates after they retire and they become hermits and homebodies; your life can feel "over" once you're in this final phase, so what will you do next? Well, some people volunteer and others take on new hobbies. Retirement can impact your identity in obvious ways.

Not all retirees are depressed about their state of being, of course, but when you are bummed, Spirit tells me that it dampens your soul. Those who grieve a loss in routine have likely gone from having a high-profile job and stimulating schedule to going to the local deli for an egg sandwich and lottery tickets. That can feel pretty ho-hum. But you should know by now that Spirit and I encourage you to see the opportunity in this loss and to *add* something to your life that wasn't there before. You've worked too hard all your life to not enjoy this next stage!

MIXED FEELINGS ARE NORMAL

Even if part of you welcomes the freedom of retirement, you might still suffer multiple losses: you can lose your identity as a working person, your status in the world, your income, and your sense of purpose. You might not even realize this is happening; little by little, these losses can sneak up on you over time. And if your life does feel less meaningful, it's easy to swing into depression because you're leaving behind valuable parts of yourself that you've come to depend on. Instead of feeling weighed down by the pressure of retirement living, Spirit wants you to focus on honoring the years you spent in your job; this will make it easier to let them go because you'll feel proud of yourself rather than regretful that you've moved on to a new stage.

My cousin John retired as a police officer at the age of forty-eight and knows exactly how it feels to welcome retirement with mixed emotions, which include feeling a sense of pride for all that he's done. John became a police officer with the New York City Police Department when he was twenty-one. He loved the action—"I had a front row seat to the greatest show on earth," he told me. After three and a half years, he changed police departments for a higher salary. After five years, he decided to leave patrol duties to work in the headquarters of his department. He also became a union rep at that time. Finally, John was asked to join the unit that tested drunk drivers. "I became an expert in that field and ran the unit," John remembered. "I tested drunk drivers, trained police officers, repaired the scientific instruments, calibrated them, taught officers how to use them, trained new prosecutors, and testified in court almost daily. The unit ran 24/7. I also moved up the ranks in the union. I became a member of the Board of Governors."

John made the decision to retire early, and quickly—three months from the day that he decided to leave to the day he retired. "Initially, I felt relieved to go," he said. "I felt elated that I would soon be free. The stress that I was under every day would soon be gone. The physical exhaustion and health issues from having to work sixty-five hours a week would be gone too. I would finally be a greater part of my children's lives." However, as his retirement day approached, John became anxious. "I began to question my decision to leave the life, identity, and career I'd known for the greater part of my adulthood," he said. Though the adjustment felt daunting, it turned out to be bittersweet. "My life isn't as hectic, which can be good and bad at times," he said. "Overall though, I feel more peaceful and relaxed. I'm taking time to enjoy life. I travel the world and do things on my terms."

Mantra: Don't just start a new chapter; open a new book. Change is good!

But John also misses a lot about his job. "I miss parts of my routine," he said, "and the fact that my job was regimented. I miss my co-workers most. We were like a family." John was able to gradually ease out of employment, which helped him adapt to his new lifestyle. "I was lucky," he said. "Being so important to the DWI program, I was required to show up for court trials after my retirement. This went on for over two years. I was in court three to five days a week. I believe that eased my transition. I still got to see my co-workers weekly and was still treated as one of them."

Eventually, full-on retirement affected John's status and income and changed his sense of purpose. "My status was diminished. As an older co-worker once said to me, 'When you're out, you're out,'" John said. "My income was also cut by more than half. So yes, I miss the money I made. I've had to cut back on some of my lifestyle. I never lost my sense of purpose; it's just different. I've always been a problem solver but still find ways to keep busy every day. I have many other interests, friends, and activities outside the police department."

Though doing less in a day and setting his own pace has its ups and downs, John can't help but miss the action sometimes. "I described my life to people like this: Every morning, I'm like the clown in the circus who climbs into that giant cannon and gets shot across three rings. I never know how much powder they're going to use each day, and I pray they set up the net in the right place." And while John hasn't experienced depression or anxiety since leaving, he said he does know cops who have spiraled downward after retirement because they loved their job so much.

Though John left his duties behind, he also left a part of himself at his job—but in the best way. "I was always charged with great responsibility. I had to keep the program and lab I built running with no mistakes," he told me. With retirement nearing, he'd searched the police department to find an officer who would adhere to the same level of high, scientific standards that he did, and even strive to improve upon the program he'd built. John found just that officer and trained him to follow in his footsteps, which in my opinion, was a tall order. "I have left a great part of me behind in a legacy," he said. What more can you ask for than that?

PREP AHEAD

As you lead up to retirement, Spirit says you should do what you can to prepare for this transition and secure a healthy future for yourself: take care of expensive doctor's appointments, meet with financial planners, decide where you can affordably live—that kind of thing. You should also plan how you'll spend your time so that you aren't shell-shocked and disoriented once you're in retirement mode. You might miss the bustle of a full-time job, so book up your leisure time, plan trips, and join as many clubs as you can to keep busy. Hobbies, community activities, and family events will help fill the holes that your job left behind. You might also think about what brings you purpose and how you can continue pursuing your passion outside of a workplace.

Redefine what it means to be productive; you're no longer recruiting clients or bringing in a top salary, but maybe how many golf games you play a week or dinners you host a month will become new benchmarks of fulfillment. My friend Anna is newly retired, and although she felt she had too much time on her hands when she first moved to Florida to start this phase of her life, she is now happily busy with barre classes, mahjong groups, trivia nights, and pool parties at the golf club in town. It took her a few months to meet friends, whom she now affectionately refers to as her "tribe." Her daughter recently needed surgery, and Anna was able to fly to Connecticut to help take care of her toddler son while her daughter recovered. Anna never could have done this in her old job as a professor, and she was so grateful that retirement allowed her this freedom.

"You have to find your people, your activities, a new lifestyle and just go with it," she said. "It's a big change from my life before, but different doesn't mean worse. It's actually much better for me in a lot of ways, but I had to make smart choices so that I would love my life again. I couldn't wait for retirement to present these opportunities to me first."

You can also invest time in the hobbies and organizations you once merely dabbled in. Perfect your watercolor skills or read voraciously on a subject that fascinates you. Volunteer for a cause you're passionate about. My father does this as a volunteer firefighter, a water commissioner, a member of the community council, a fifth-degree Knight of Columbus, and more. He does so much, in fact, that he's always being honored for how engaged he is in our Long Island community. As for my mom, she spends a lot of time volunteering at her church. These activities keep them busy and their minds occupied. I'm always impressed with how fulfilled they are for two people with time on their hands! Sometimes I forget that my parents are even retired; it can be hard to get my mom on the phone and my dad to visit, especially when he's occupied with his tomato garden. Most important, my parents' full schedules make them feel happy and give them a sense of purpose each day. They keep moving and socializing, and they keep their spirits up—so their brains and bodies stay as stimulated and youthful as possible.

I often think about what retirement will be like for me, and my mind immediately concludes that I will likely *never* retire! I love what I do, and I can't imagine stopping. People will always need the gift of healing. Will I slow down and travel less? Write fewer books? Of course. I might not hustle as hard, but I won't ever stop moving. I'll simply reach the next phase of my career, with a lighter schedule and plenty of time to rest. I'll make even more time for my family, and spend it with my kids and grandkids, if I have them. To be honest with you, that sounds pretty good to me *right now*! Who's scared of retirement? I say, bring it on!

Try to experience this next phase not as a letdown or scary step, but as an adventure to be celebrated and enjoyed. It might sound strange to expect to grieve alongside the freedom and happiness of retirement, but Spirit says it's a stage of unknown. You're embarking on a journey that's the complete opposite of what you once considered familiar and normal. That's exciting!

Good Mourning

In a journal, make three columns: in the first, write down the best part of your busy workday; in the second, describe how that activity made you feel; and in the third, suggest a new activity that elicits the same feelings as your work activity. For example, if you loved the social aspect of answering phones at work, write "answering phones" in the first column. Then in the second, write "I liked helping strangers." In the third, think of an activity that would create a similar satisfaction of helping strangers—maybe volunteering at the front desk of a local library or on a suicide prevention hotline. The goal is to fill your time with activities that make you happy to start each day.

16

ON LOSING AN ARGUMENT

Believe it or not, you can experience grief when you lose an argument. It's more than feeling pissed off that the other person had the last say—it's a jumble of emotions that make you feel defeated, as if your opinions don't matter, and that your feelings weren't validated or clearly heard. It can leave you with an emptiness in your heart and a pit in your stomach. And if a fight ends badly, even the person who seemed to come out on top can feel like they've lost their integrity while hashing things out. Cruel words can be said by all; repressed feelings can fly everywhere. Everyone knows an argument can get messy and painful, but when it's all said and done, there also can be a lot of grief and loss to deal with afterward. Cleanup on aisle nine!

After you've lost an argument you might go through your day feeling ready to blow or collapse into tears at any moment, because this loss essentially takes away your voice and any sense of control you might have once felt over the situation at hand. When you don't feel that your side of the story was heard, respected, or valued, it's more than an annoying, missed opportunity—it's a real insult.

The other person might as well have covered their ears and cried, "Lalalalala, I can't heeear you!" It's that much of a blatant disregard.

WHAT DOES IT MEAN TO BE RIGHT?

Spirit says the best way to deal with losing an argument is to recognize that just because you may not seem to come out on top doesn't mean you aren't right. Who determines who wins or loses a fight, anyway? Just because a person argues an opinion louder or harder than you doesn't mean that their view is the end-all conclusion to the discussion. It just means that maybe you agreed to disagree or call a truce to preserve whatever peace was left. Sometimes taking the high road is better than winning a fight. To the soul, Spirit says handling a rough situation with dignity means more than being "right." You don't need the last word; chances are, your life doesn't depend on this resolution. Sometimes losing an argument and apologizing when you don't mean it can even save a relationship, and that preservation means more than one-upping someone you care about.

Experts say that the best way to enter into an argument is to view it as a platform to hear the other person's point of view, find areas of agreement, ask thoughtful questions, know when to admit you're wrong, focus on your best interests, and ultimately try to resolve the conflict before it blows up into a painful memory that you can't soon forget. The focus shouldn't be on convincing the other person to agree with your position by talking louder or shaming them into listening and then finally waving the white flag.

Your goal in any argument or heated discussion should be to find a peaceful resolution—one where you both understand the other person's POV and where the relationship remains in good standing because you've decided to put it before your need to be correct. Forget pride and winning; focus on arguing toward a goal that will enhance your relationship and bond.

Learning how to argue and to talk to another person in a way that puts the relationship above the almighty ego is what Spirit wants for us at the end of the day. After all, Spirit says that our souls tell us when we've made a mistake. There's no need to prove that we're right or wrong because our conscience and inner voice will let us know. If you and the other person take time to reflect on your words and conclusions, your opinions will find a way to align because your hearts will be in the right place—they'll want to be on the same page.

I know I've had arguments and disagreements that I felt like I "lost" because they left me feeling like crap, but what was really happening was that I was more focused on being heard than on finding a peaceful resolution. Sometimes I'll explain something to my daughter, Victoria, and she'll think I'm getting mad, but I'm really just arguing my point with a very loud passion—and there's a difference! In the end, we always make nice since we have a bond that doesn't allow us to stay frustrated with each other for long.

NO REGRETS!

When Spirit talks about losing an argument, they repeatedly drill down on how important it is to avoid saying something you will later regret or want to take back but can't. You don't want to be so intent on getting your feelings across that you're hurtful, and then wish you'd never said what you did. You also don't want to be so afraid of speaking your truth that you regret what you *didn't* say. To put it another way, you don't want to look back and feel sorry for the way that your argument went down and feel shame, guilt, or regrets around the choice to fight at all.

This topic reminds me of my friend Jill, whose ex-husband John committed suicide at the age of forty-five. Jill and John's love story was a long one; they began dating when they were seventeen, though he'd had a crush on her since kindergarten. Yet a week before John passed, the two argued about the fact that he was an alcoholic and abusive toward Jill and her two kids, Shana and Jon. John had two DUIs and was about to go to court and possibly serve time in jail.

"At the time of the fight, I felt that my kids and I were justified to get so upset," Jill told me. "We'd had a few years of drama—a lot of arguments, tears, yelling, and abuse." The family stood up to John for the first time about his behavior and addiction and decided to become estranged from him. John killed himself five days later because, as Jill believes, he felt "alone and desperate" without them.

"At times, I feel that had we not made the decision to cut John off, there may have been a chance that he would have lived. But I realize that's just me blaming myself," Jill said. "I spent my entire relationship with him trying to prevent the inevitable. There were many years when he didn't drink, but after losing us, he went on a downward spiral. He was a good man, just very sick." Jill said that she'd always tried to prevent and control situations that would shield her and her family from John's self-destructive behavior, but it was getting increasingly difficult. "I did everything I could to try to save him," she said, "and I often lost myself in the process."

Jill refuses to regret her argument with John and said there were no winners or losers in their fight because John died, and with that, everyone ultimately lost. To cope with the tragedy, Jill appreciates her two children and remembers "a beautiful life before John's addiction stole it from us. He was a wonderful husband, dad, and friend. He loved me his entire life." Jill also tries to focus on how much she did for John while he was alive, including making him feel welcome in her extended family. "We were all John had," she said. "His family was very dysfunctional, and he tried so hard. He loved us. He just didn't know how to love himself. I showed him what a real, loving family was. He was close to my mom and dad, as well."

This is all to say that Jill forgives herself for that last argument but will never forget it. "It was the last time that my daughter and I spoke to him," Jill said. "But I can't let it define who I am and what we were. I was fighting for the four of us, and I tell my children that we can't be angry because then we'll lose our past, present, and future. I will always keep John's life as a part of ours, and he will not be forgotten. One of the last things he said to me was, 'I tried to be everything I wanted to be, and what you wanted and believed I could be, but I couldn't do it.'"

Mantra: Today I will pay attention to my words. I will say what I mean and mean what I say.

Perhaps because Jill and her family aren't burdened by shame or regret anymore, John's soul is free to guide, love, and protect his family without restriction from the other side. For instance, the morning of John's memorial, Jill said his favorite song by AC/DC came on the radio during their ride to church. "It gave us a feeling of hope that John's soul was with us," said Jill. Her daughter Shana, a teacher at the school where Jill and John graduated, also experienced a remarkable event. A week into the school year, she decided to clean the nine desks in her classroom. She nearly freaked out when she saw that one had the words "Jill loves John" still etched in it—the desk dated back to the time when one of her parents sat in it! Of the hundreds of desks in that school, what are the odds that their daughter would get that desk in her room? That was definitely a message from John, letting Shana know that his love lives on in this world.

Good Mourning

Think about the last time you felt you lost an argument. In a journal, draw two columns—one for all the good points you made during the argument, and one for all the valid points the other person made. Make a list of them. When you look at the points now, who do you feel "won" the fight—and does it really matter? Of course not. What matters is that you recognize what both parties are saying and respect it. After evaluating both sides of the story, draw a huge *X* over the columns. It's time to put it to rest.

17

ON LOSING TRUST

*E*ach betrayal begins with trust" is one of my favorite quotations attributed to the German theologian Martin Luther. It's also a lyric in the Phish song "Farmhouse," for those who know it! No matter what your reference, this timeless quotation really hits home if you've ever had someone stomp all over your level of trust.

Broken promises made by a person whom you rely on, and believe in, are some of the hardest obstacles to overcome. This loss cuts deep, and I honestly don't know whether there's a worse feeling. To have your trust compromised or even secrets exposed makes you feel that you're not valued. It causes you to act guarded. You have trouble healing from the break and difficulty believing in others who claim to be supportive of you. It shakes the very foundation of a relationship and causes you to question everything. After a significant letdown, it's hard to trust yourself, or even God.

At the core of all these trust issues is the belief that those who you thought were rooting for you, never were. Losing trust means yielding to the fact that you've been lied to and that deception is at the core of your relationship. It's a very painful cross to bear.

SPIRIT, ON TRUST ISSUES

When I channel the topic of trust, Spirit has quite a few things to say. First, the issue of trust always comes up when I sit with a client who is disappointed that someone didn't leave money to them in a will. They'll say that they trusted the person who died to do the "right thing" and then felt let down. To this, Spirit often says that we shouldn't focus on material goods and instead should value the memories we shared with someone. Second, the topic of trust arises when Spirit asks that we all trust God and have faith knowing that there are souls on the other side that are meant to guide, love, and protect us. Guidance by these powerful souls is our birthright, so we should invite them to share a trustworthy bond with us. Third, Spirit reinforces that when we feel betrayed, we must remember that we aren't at fault and aren't responsible for other people's actions, no matter how hard they try to peg their bad behavior on us.

Spirit says it's important to untangle yourself from trust issues as fast as you can because they will kill your soul.

My guides emphasize that when you've been burned a lot, you'll have trouble trusting others. When this happens, you need to lean on spiritual beings whom you know are true blue and trustworthy—God, angels, your guides, and loved ones' souls in Heaven. You'll never have to doubt whether you should place your trust in these celestial beings, because they'll always be there for you in the most honest and earnest way.

Spirit also says that you should try your best to recover from the loss of trust by taking small steps toward regaining your confidence in the person or situation that has betrayed you. It's a silly example, but think about how you might lose trust in dogs if one unexpectedly bit you. If you prayed on this, Spirit would put opportunities in your path for you to regain your trust of dogs, and it would be up to you to take those opportunities. So, you might encounter a dog on the street and start by letting that dog smell your hand. Then you might visit a dog at a shelter and pet it while someone else holds it so that you can feel comfortable and safe while getting to know the animal. Then you might ask to hold a neighbor's puppy while the owner stands nearby. Finally, you might take a friend's gentle dog for a walk and regain your confidence in dogs that don't bite.

My client Valencia suffered from enormous trust issues after her wife Shannon got pregnant behind Valencia's back. The couple already had two children together, using a sperm donor they'd chosen together, and had agreed that their family was complete. However, years later, Shannon decided that she wanted another baby, although Valencia did not. This didn't stop Shannon from choosing a new donor on her own and going through the process of getting pregnant with the help of a fertility clinic. She didn't tell Valencia about this deceitful maneuver until she was three months pregnant and beginning to show.

Valencia felt deeply hurt and betrayed, although she felt she had no choice but to support her wife, whom she loved very much. The couple agreed to raise their beautiful third child together, but Valencia could never get over the fact that her wife had gotten pregnant without telling her. It was a selfish move that could have broken the relationship. Valencia ultimately forgave Shannon for what she did, but she can't forget it.

And so every day, Valencia has chosen to move on from that enormous betrayal of trust with baby steps that slowly reinforce her faith in the relationship and Shannon's future honesty. Valencia prayed that Shannon would grant her opportunities to allow her to soften toward Shannon, despite how hurt and betrayed Valencia felt. Sure enough, Shannon made small gestures—a little at a time—to encourage Valencia to trust her again. First, Shannon apologized, and Valencia accepted that apology. Then, she made little promises that she said she'd keep—small things like emptying the dishwasher when she said she would or taking the kids to the mall so Valencia could have some time to herself—which showed Valencia that Shannon was genuinely interested in making things right. Valencia then welcomed Shannon's offer to plan a romantic vacation for just the two of them to renew the intimacy that had been compromised by their trust issues. Over time, and with increasing effort, Valencia began to heal and take Shannon at her word. It took more than a year, but the two have since resolved the issue and are a happy family again.

TRADING TRUST FOR PAIN

We can lose trust in all kinds of ways—in people, in our bodies, or in love—and all of these can be extremely painful. In a way, the pain that we feel when our trust has been broken tells us that we're vulnerable and capable of caring, which can be a good thing because it shows us that we are ethical humans with well-intentioned, beating hearts. And so, when we're hurt, our trust has the capacity to feel violated.

When you're dealing with trust issues, you should also watch out for toxic thoughts that creep into your mind—like the fact that you should be over the betrayal by now, that things will never be the same, that life is unfair, and that it's all your fault. Spirit says that these are not helpful intrusions and can only make things worse for you. Talk about mind drama! The last thing you need is to feed your insecurities because of another person's lies.

A woman I know named Annette was married to a man who lied compulsively, treated her badly when she was sick, made changes to their will and life insurance policy behind her back, and told untrue stories about Annette to their friends. The couple is now divorcing, but when they initially moved from New York to Florida, Annette gave up a lot to be with her husband—including great financial stability.

Before moving, Annette had a beautiful home, rental income, and no debt other than a mortgage. "I left my job as an educational sign language interpreter for the deaf because my husband convinced me that he wanted a life with me. I gave up my great-paying state job to relocate to Florida with him," she said. "I gave up my seniority and the pension money I would have gotten had I stayed twenty years—I was only one and a half years away from this. I was proud of what I had achieved on my own." Now, Annette is able to find only basic paying jobs, and when her divorce is finalized, she will have only a small alimony on which to live because of her husband's modest salary. "I'll never own a home again. I can't afford a decent apartment," she said. "I'll struggle financially. I worked and fought hard to achieve what I had. In trusting this man, I lost it all."

Annette's husband first turned on her when she became sick with a curious thyroid imbalance. He said her symptoms were psychosomatic, he refused to see doctors with her when she was searching for a diagnosis, and he gossiped about her to friends. "Had I not gotten sick, I never would have known my husband was the selfish, deceitful, and unreliable person that he actually is," she said. "A true test of a person's character is when things go wrong, not when everything is perfect. Running when things get tough is cowardly and childish. God gave me the gift of seeing the truth in the man who I am married to. I now see that he's no man at all."

Annette's husband lied to neighbors about her health and made a chaotic scene when he visited her in the hospital, where the nursing staff had to toss him out. When Annette needed surgery a few days later, he refused to take her to the hospital for the procedure. "An elderly Italian couple who I adore got up at 4:30 a.m. and drove me to the hospital," she said. "They were by my side. Not my husband." For some time, Annette tried to forgive her husband but lost friends in the process. "They didn't understand my love and loyalty to him," she said. "They feel he is a cruel, sick person. It's hard for them to stand by, watching me endure this nonsense. I've pushed friends away because I'm ashamed that I allowed this to happen to me."

Annette's husband also tried to alienate her from new friends. "He told people that I was unstable and said he didn't know this until he lived with me," Annette said. "This was a lie because he lived with me in New York before we moved here, and I was fine. He also told his four kids that I was putting him through hell and that I wouldn't allow him to have contact with them. He told neighbors with whom I was starting to develop friendships how I wouldn't allow a relationship with his children and that I had turned his family against him and had them wrapped around my finger. The truth is, his family doesn't speak to him, are not the type to be manipulated, and are so supportive of me."

To Annette, her husband's repeated betrayals denied everything their marriage should have stood for—"Namely, his vows to protect me and build me up, not knock me down. Telling half-truths and lies, though, was the ultimate betrayal," she said. "When you love someone so much, you don't expect that or see it coming." She said that no matter how she tries to reach out to him, her husband has no empathy whatsoever.

Mantra: Because I trust myself, and trust in God, all things are possible.

"It's the worst feeling to grieve the loss of trust," she continued. "It's as if you're mourning a death. It's hard to wrap your head around the idea that someone you adored could be this monster. It consumes every minute of your day and rips you out of your sleep." Through this betrayal, Annette feels she's lost part of herself. "I don't feel whole anymore. I don't trust myself. I'm ashamed that I didn't see clearly," she said. "I've become very depressed. I find socializing difficult. It's always on my mind. It's like a disease that I'm unable to cure."

If there's an upside to any of this, Annette feels it's that she has grown stronger in her religious faith. "I'm closer to God than I have ever been. I made the mistake of running away from God when I should have been running toward Him," she told me. "I've learned we all have crosses to carry. I've learned who my true friends and family are. God has blessed me with angels during this difficult time. I read the Bible, attend Mass, talk with my priests, and make it a point to be kinder to strangers."

Because of her faithfulness, I know that God will bless

Annette—as He will bless everyone who suffers from a loss of trust. It's one of the most difficult losses we face, but also one of the most rewarding to overcome because it requires believing in yourself, first and foremost. When you can grow beyond the damage that another person has done to you, you win.

Good Mourning

The goal of this exercise is to reestablish your ability to trust others and trust your own judgment above all else. When a person betrays your trust, it's easy to start doubting yourself and your ability to make good decisions. I'd like you to make one leap of faith and trust that the outcome will be positive. So perhaps it's hard to believe that a new car mechanic will give you a fair estimate on fixing your car. I'd like you to trust that he isn't taking you for a ride and put your faith in his service, no questions asked. Or maybe it's tricky to trust that your sister is telling the truth when she says you look great in a certain outfit. Believe that you look amazing and thank her for the compliment! What about when your child says you're the best parent ever, and you internally shake your head? Have faith that you're the bee's knees in your kid's eyes! The more you exercise your ability to take people at their word, the easier it will be for you to trust those who are closest to you and your own ability to see through other people's nonsense.

18

ON LOSING A
SPECIAL OBJECT

When you lose a special object—whether it's a piece of jewelry or clothing, or something else from your home—it can break your heart, especially if it belonged to a loved one who has passed. It might be a family heirloom or antique that's meaningful to you, or a brand-new gift from someone you care about. When that object goes missing, it can feel like a piece of you has gone away too. Yet no matter how special such things are, Spirit insists that these are physical objects that will not replace the actual thoughts and feelings you've attached to them. Those warm sentiments are what we should focus on, not the material things themselves.

Even so, I personally find that I become very attached to objects. My three favorite things—my favorite black sweatshirt, my favorite black dress, and my favorite duffel bag—I take wherever I go. All of these items make me feel confident and give me a sense of security and familiarity. The sweatshirt makes me feel like I'm wearing a cozy hug from home; the dress makes me look good, feel good, and act confidently when I'm in public (even if I've put on a few pounds); and my favorite duffel makes me feel safe when I travel, which is important because I used to be afraid to go anywhere. The security that these objects provide is part history, part superstition, but 100 percent real and helpful for me.

MISSING OBJECTS, EMPTY FEELINGS

When you grieve the loss of a special object, you can become filled with a mixed bag of emotions. You might get mad at yourself for misplacing the object or sad that you can't show it off and tell its story. You might feel disappointed or even depressed because you no longer have what you felt was a symbol of another person's love, devotion, or good taste. And when you lose an object that belonged to a loved one who has passed, you might feel more distant from that person's energy because wearing their watch or pin made you feel close to their soul.

I don't sense energy through objects (metals, certain fabrics, and woods hold it very well), but some people can. And when they do, the pain of losing a special object can feel twice as profound. These people aren't imagining that they feel closer to their loved one by having the item with them; they actually feel their soul's presence when they handle or wear it. Wild, huh?

Spirit says you get so attached to things because they represent memories of a place, friend, loved one, and/or feeling. The more you wear or use or carry the item, the deeper the attachment gets. I'll never forget when I thought I lost my Gram's wedding ring. I frantically looked for it and tore apart my safe, because Victoria wanted to wear it to her engagement party. Spirit showed me, however, that it was already in my daughter's ring dish—thank Heaven!—and boy, was I relieved to find it there. Even I'm guilty of caring about family heirlooms, mostly because I love the memories that are attached to them. You can never take those away from me.

Without your special objects, you might also feel a loss of identity. You might worry that your memories will fade away. My friend Jen lost her laptop, for instance, on a recent vacation to Puerto Rico. Losing it made Jen feel vulnerable and exposed, because it contained her deepest secrets, favorite photos, best stories, necessary work documents, and ideas for future projects. She couldn't imagine walking through life without this necessity, as it was always like a confidant for her, through good times and bad. Losing her laptop also made Jen worry that the memories she stored there would be gone forever and that she'd lose touch with the person she once was when she wouldn't be able to look back and reminisce. Jen was hoping to pass down various files and photos from her laptop to her children in the future, and now this wasn't an option for her.

Mantra: I cherish what I've lost, but I'm grateful for what I have left.

Jen grieved long and hard for her lost writings, and though she bought a new laptop to replace her old one, she isn't trying to recount and rewrite what she has lost. Instead, she's simply moving forward with fresh thoughts and ideas from a new life, starting over without looking back.

Come to think of it, I know people who decorate their homes

and surround themselves with meaningful memorabilia. Everything is antiques and heirlooms, grandma's sofa and a great-aunt's quilt. Sentimental items are what qualify something to be a home in their eyes, so losing any of those items means starting over.

Nobody likes to lose things because it could mean having to learn to let go. My client Tina recently had to get rid of half the items in her home, many of which were of sentimental value, because they were exposed to toxic mold and the chemicals used to treat the infestation. "With each chair, settee, and pillow that I had to throw out, I felt like a piece of me went with it," Tina said. "Even though I replaced all of my favorite things with new and beautiful décor, it doesn't feel the same to me. My new home doesn't feel like the other house I'd worked so hard to design. It lacks the history and integrity. It lacks the memories and stories that made each piece so special to me." Tina feels like she's living in a stranger's home now. "I have to keep telling myself that my new pieces will become heirlooms for my family someday," Tina said. "It will take time to feel okay about what I've lost. I need to focus on how my new space is healthier and can make me just as happy."

MOVING TOWARD ACCEPTANCE

The best way to deal with the loss of sentimental items is to move toward acceptance as quickly as you can. Realize that memories are not within the physical thing but in your mind and heart. You are still you, and you are not less of a person without the thing you've lost. Know that nobody can take from you your memories and what those objects represented—the relationships, experiences, friendships, and more. Accept that the item is gone and look forward to making new memories and creating new heir-looms with those you love who are all around you.

My client Anna's mother Marie died from a devastating auto-immune disease called scleroderma, and the two women became very close when Marie was battling this debilitating illness. Anna and Marie spent almost every day together—first, when Marie was able, they'd go to lunch or the movies together; and then, when Marie was practically bedridden, they'd talk about her memories and what she missed most about her life. As they did, Anna would always admire her mom's beautiful wedding ring set—a substantial diamond engagement ring that Anna's older sister would have one day and a simple diamond wedding band. Though Anna never asked, she often hoped that she would inherit the band.

Sure enough, when Marie was on her deathbed, she told Anna how grateful she was for always being with her when she was in need. "She took off her wedding band and put it in my hand," Anna said. "It was this modest diamond band that she truly cher-ished as a symbol of her and my dad's love for one another. She wanted me to have it; it would always link us together and be a loving remembrance of how much she loved me."

Anna wore her mom's ring for a number of years with her own wedding rings. She looked at it and turned it around on her fin-ger often; it was a talisman that connected her to her mom. "I felt safe, protected, and loved as long as I was wearing that ring," Anna said. Also at that time, Anna's sixteen-year-old daughter, Gena, was having a challenging time at home, in school, with her boyfriend—and especially with her mom, Anna. Although the two had always been like oil and water, Anna loved her dearly. But Anna felt she couldn't persuade Gena of her love and wanted to do something special to prove her devotion. So she gave Gena her mom's ring to cherish. Anna hoped that Gena would feel the same way Anna had felt when wearing her mom's ring: safe, protected, and loved. Gena was thrilled to receive it and promised to take good care of this family heirloom.

Over the next few months, Gena wore her grandmother's ring all the time. She went to school with it, bathed with it, played soccer with it. One day, however, Anna noticed that her mom's ring wasn't on Gena's finger. When she asked her about it, Gena gave her mom a look that said, *Mom, I've done something, again, to disappoint you.* "My heart sank, and my stomach got queasy," Anna told me. "I knew she'd lost my mom's ring and was afraid to tell me."

At first, Anna was angry and devastated, both by the loss of the ring and the fact that Gena could have been so irresponsible with it. She then remembered, however, how Marie once had told her, when she lost her pinky ring, to simply pray to Saint Anthony, the patron saint of lost objects, for help. "So pray to him, I did," said Anna. "Again, and again, and again. But we didn't find the ring. Gena retraced her steps, but to no avail. The only other place she had worn her ring the week she lost it was in a friend's extra-large hot tub. Forget that. The ring was forever lost."

Thinking back, Anna wonders about this time in her and Gena's lives. Was she meant to give Gena her mom's ring? Was Gena meant to lose it? Was this part of a bigger picture, a grander design? "I do believe it was," said Anna. "In retrospect, that incident allowed us to openly talk to one another about our feelings, past misconceptions, and future as mother and daughter."

A few weeks later, Gena asked Anna to open her hand, and she put a very small box into it. Inside was a delicate, beautiful pinky ring carved with the figure of an angel. "Gena wanted me to have a symbol of her love, since she'd lost my mom's ring that I loved so much," Anna said. "Ever since, Gena and I have had a more open, loving relationship. We didn't really need my mother's wedding band; we had something more powerful, something which would never be lost or replaced—we had our new relationship, symbolized by the new ring. We both felt my mom's presence very strongly at that moment. I believe my mom wanted us to know that we had her spirit with us forever, and perhaps Saint Anthony helped us find something more important than a material object—he helped us find acceptance, and a fresh perspective on our relationship."

Spirit says it's easy to get upset when an object goes missing but to maintain perspective and always keep the faith. Even if the missing object never turns up, God will provide you with a satisfying response to your grief, whether it's a sign, a symbol, or a nudge to your intuition to replace the object with something similarly meaningful. But in the end, Spirit's plan for you rarely involves material goods; they are simply representations of the love you hold in your heart. This contains much more value than all the heirlooms and antiques in the world.

Good Mourning

Buy a special box that's big enough to store three special objects. Line it with pretty paper and then place your finest mementos inside. Though there's always a chance that these items can get lost, keeping them in a designated place will help them stay as safe as possible. Storing them this way will also allow you to pass them on to family with the reverence they deserve.

17

ON LOSING A BODY PART

When you lose a body part, it understandably feels like a piece of you has gone missing, both literally and figuratively. It's no wonder that you experience all the stages of grief here—from shock, to anger, to depression, and everything in between. You feel betrayed by various institutions and figures, including God, and wonder why such a thing would happen to you. Whether you lost a body part to a mastectomy, amputation, or other type of surgery, in the end, it doesn't matter. Your loss is your loss—and whatever meaning it holds for you will define how much pain you'll go through. Losing a breast can be just as harrowing as losing a kidney or a finger, depending on what your relationship is to the body part, how it came to be removed, and what your emotional experience was around the surgery, incident, or accident. As with all losses, there is no hierarchy when it comes to this grief. We all feel our pain 100 percent.

I can relate to the loss of a body part, as I witnessed and sensed the effect that it had on a close family member when I was young. Back in the 1970s, Gram's left breast was removed because of breast cancer. She opted for a prosthesis, which she discreetly tucked into her bra, and often cleverly wore striped sweaters so that she could line up the prosthesis on her left side with her natural breast on her right.

Mom said that Gram was a modest woman and kept her feelings about this surgery to herself, though I intuited that Gram felt insecure and uncomfortable at times about her new figure. I remember this impression so clearly, even though Mom said that if Gram ever felt insecure or less of a woman, she wouldn't have shared those feelings. Yet I could sense that Gram felt self-conscious at times, which I think was normal—especially back then, when women didn't talk as openly about this intimate cancer, and its related grief, as we do now.

WHERE DID I GO?

When you lose a body part, Spirit says you initially feel disoriented because you don't recognize how your changed body looks, functions, and feels. Your figure no longer feels like your own, even if only one small part of it has been altered. Its overall landscape has changed, and you notice how it affects your looks and how you function all day long. Your routines become different—how you get dressed, bathe, move through the world, socialize . . . the list goes on. For instance, if you lose a leg and have a prosthesis in its place, you may not want to wear dresses or initially be able to go dancing the same way that you used to. If you have a mastectomy, you may no longer be able to wear a bathing suit without feeling self-conscious. You might feel less attractive to your partner or have less of a sex drive. All of these changes, challenges, and demands—coming at you all at once—can feel overwhelming.

As a result, you might feel isolated and withdrawn, and Spirit says that's okay. Sometimes you need to be alone to fully absorb your loss and digest how your life has changed. When something happens to me, I'm the opposite of withdrawn, but that's just how I cope. When I had a brace on my leg from the accident in Hawaii, I told everyone in line at the store about my business! I wanted people to understand why I walked in a funny way, and it helped me to normalize my disability by talking about it.

I also liked wearing the brace because it gave others a visual cue about what was going on; if I were grieving the loss of, say, my uterus from a hysterectomy, I might be struggling but other people wouldn't know why. They might judge me without knowing my story. I realize that I didn't lose a body part in Hawaii, but I get some of the issues you might be going through because of what I went through. I felt like I was missing my leg for a long time.

Spirit says that more than any other emotion, anger is dominant here because this feeling is simply fear turned outward, and losing a body part is a scary thing. You might get frustrated with God for not protecting you and even relatives who've passed on their "bad genes" to you. You might become furious at doctors for putting you through grueling treatments or not catching the condition right away that led to your situation. If you lose a body part because of an accident, it's natural to get angry at the person who caused it—and if the accident was your fault, you might get angry at yourself, or even at the dumb deer that suddenly jumped out in the road.

You might not necessarily feel the need to blame, but you do want to direct your fury at someone or something to help make sense of your situation. This lasts until restlessness and confusion set in, then depression and insecurity. The whole situation can feel overwhelmingly unfair, and you'll feel like a shadow of your former self. According to one study, for example, most women need two years before feeling resolved about the loss of a breast. Spirit says that's a sizable grief process if ever there were one.

THE DRAMA OF TRAUMA

The loss of a body part is deeply rooted in trauma, and you can be easily triggered when events, TV shows, otherwise ordinary errands, and even certain seasons or holidays bring up memories and pain. You might even think you've reached acceptance, breathe a sigh of relief, and then something else will set you back and trigger your sense of loss all over again. Your triggers will be unique to your situation, though there are some commonalities. Shopping can be a difficult trigger for a lot of people who've lost a body part, as can intimacy with a partner or spouse. Going to the doctor might cause you to remember the moment you became ill.

Avoidance can be a coping strategy, as can developing related rituals to circumvent situations that upset you—think: covering mirrors while getting dressed, undressing in the dark, minimizing bathing time, and avoiding seeing yourself naked as much as possible. You might do all of these things to avoid retraumatizing yourself when you are confronted by your body's new state.

When you encounter traumatic triggers, it's natural to freeze up, and Spirit says to take baby steps when coming back into a healthy mindset. If shopping is hard, buy your clothes online for a while. Then when you feel ready, go for a walk in the mall, but don't shop. Later that week, find a few pieces of clothing and hold them up to you without trying them on. Eventually, you'll shore up the courage to buy clothes that make you feel great without feeling afraid of the process.

My client Jolie had a partial hysterectomy in 2007 and suffered from related grief for a long time. Jolie struggles with a painful condition called endometriosis, in which tissue similar to that which lines the uterus grows outside of it. She was set to have surgery, but the day before she was scheduled to go in, her surgeon told her that she also had adenomyosis, a condition in which the inner lining of the uterus breaks through its muscle wall. Because of this painful one-two punch, her doctors now recommended a hysterectomy—and the suggestion floored Jolie. She almost didn't go through with it, but during the last few days of her father's life, he had told her to take care of herself and to get whatever surgeries she needed to feel better. Almost two months after his death, Jolie found a necklace he had given her in her purse next to information she had picked up about the surgery, so she took that as a sign that it was safe to proceed with the procedure.

Despite this undeniable sign, Jolie felt traumatized after surgery. With her cervix and part of her ovaries gone as well, she felt that integral parts of her were missing. "A lot of this was because I was relatively young—in my early thirties—with no children, and it was a time when all of my peers were becoming parents and I still wasn't one," she told me. "I was also constantly exposed to pregnancy announcements and complaints about parenthood on Facebook and at social events." What's more, Jolie found that going for medical checkups triggered her because one of the first questions that she would be asked on intake forms was when her last menstrual period was, and she hadn't fully processed not having one at all! "I'd wish there were a way that this screening could be more sensitive to reproductive loss like the one I experienced," she said.

Jolie felt mostly sadness, anger, and shock after surgery, especially when she was triggered. "I used to just 'get through' my day, and allow myself to cry when I got home," she said. "Another reason the procedure was so traumatic was because I had no preparation. I traveled by plane to get to the doctors and didn't have a lot of money at the time, so I had to make a critical, life-altering decision, with no time to think. I wasn't offered any counseling." Jolie said that she felt like her wounds were reopened every time someone talked to her about building a family or assumed she was too focused on her career to start one. "I wasn't ready to talk about something so personal just yet," she said. "The few people I talked to were also relatively quick to dismiss my and my husband's feelings. It was considered taboo to discuss my traumatic experiences with my reputable surgeon in certain patient forums; I was met with hostility, and it felt like blaming the victim."

A NEW NORMAL

Spirit says that people who have either lost a body part or replaced one with a prosthesis can feel that any action they take to normalize their appearance, no matter how realistic, can still make them feel like the effort doesn't represent their "real body." At that point, guilt might kick in for missing the part that was lost to the disease or incident if their life was spared because of it. I know a woman who lost part of her leg to an extensive bacterial infection and feels tremendous guilt because even though the operation saved her life, she is so upset that she no longer has her entire leg. When these conflicting emotions occur, Spirit says it's okay to feel *both* the loss and grief and the gratitude, even at the same time.

Spirit says that sometimes life just happens to us, and losing a body part can come with living on this earthly plane. Spirit suggests focusing instead on the fact that there's always a worse scenario. Perhaps you could have died from the accident or disease that took part of your body. Or maybe you lost a limb but, for instance, your face was spared from being disfigured. Find the positive. Yes, you may have to do things differently now, but maybe you can help others live a better life through your example.

Spirit says to take all the time you need to grieve, since you aren't the same physical person that you were before surgery, and you can't escape the visual proof of this—but try to shift your focus to the progress you've made and talk to people who have already been there. Find a purpose that gives your life meaning again, perhaps one that's related to your disability yet doesn't trigger your traumatic memories. Acceptance will eventually come and bring with it wisdom and character. Your mood will lift, and you may want to volunteer with organizations that make you feel more in control of your life and condition. You will regain aspects of your identity and a sense of freedom that you thought you'd lost forever. You will find new ways to reach your hopes and dreams, new definitions of normalcy, new ways of dealing with awkward conversations about your condition, and new ways to have fun when you're with loved ones.

Once you proceed to acceptance, you may feel an unexpected heap of gratitude for what you've endured. My client Robin was diagnosed in July 2018 with triple negative breast cancer, the most aggressive type, at age forty-three. She also had a genetic mutation that greatly increased the risk of her breast cancer returning after treatment, and the risk of her developing ovarian cancer. After sixteen rounds of chemotherapy, Robin finally decided to have both of her breasts removed, as well as her ovaries.

"This is the most aggressive surgery for reducing reoccurrence or another cancer," she said.

Robin said that she experienced "every feeling imaginable" after her diagnosis. In the beginning, she was thrown by shock and disbelief. "I never in a million years thought breast cancer would happen to me. Cancer happened to other people and other families," she said. "We are a family with no history of cancer. I was young, ate healthy food, exercised daily, never smoked, went for annual checkups—I was doing everything right. I was also a bit embarrassed and ashamed that this happened to me. I didn't want people to feel sorry for me and my family." After surgery, she found herself annoyed and disgusted by some people's responses, mostly men's, to her missing breasts. "They'd ask how big I'd make my breasts during reconstruction or say that at least I'd get a free boob job," she said. "There's nothing fun about having your breasts removed and reconstructed. They will never look like or feel like 'normal' breasts."

Robin couldn't believe what her body looked like during those initial days following surgery. "I had huge scars across each of my breasts, no nipples, and four drains coming out of my body—two on each side," she remembered. "Talk about humbling. My husband had to clean the drains twice a day and log the amount of fluid. I seriously didn't know how he would ever look at me the same, sexually."

Robin spent most of the first few weeks after surgery in an electric-powered reclining chair to ease the pain of getting from a sitting to standing position. "I had immediate reconstruction during the mastectomy using implants," she said. "In my case, the surgeon placed a balloonlike expander under my chest muscles to be gradually filled with saline over the course of weeks to stretch the skin. This process is extremely uncomfortable. Once expansion was complete, at about twelve weeks, I had another operation to swap out the expander for the final implant."

Mantra: My weaknesses and insecurities today will make me stronger and more confident tomorrow.

The body Robin once knew was no longer recognizable to her. "I lost all sensation in my breasts," she said. "I was no longer allowed to wear my beautiful collection of underwired bras—it would only be bralettes for the rest of my life. I was also sad about losing what these breasts represented: my femininity and being a mother. Those breasts fed my children and were such a big part of being pregnant."

To this day, Robin has to be careful with the clothes she wears. "With no sensation in my breasts, any strapless shirt, dress, or bathing suit could fall down without my knowing or feeling it," she said. "If my eyes were closed, I wouldn't even know if anyone were touching my breasts." Yet when she's dressed, no one would ever know the trauma her body has endured. It's only at night, when she lies in bed, that she can feel "suffocated by my new breasts, or lack of old ones," she noted. "I feel pressure and intense itching. I can't get comfortable. It's usually when I'm in bed that I feel my breasts, making sure there are no new lumps and bumps."

Robin experienced a great deal of trauma after her ordeal. "Seeing my new chest was a constant reminder that I had cancer and my life was forever changed," she said. Even so, Robin was thankful that losing her breasts meant her life was spared. "I know that keeping my breasts would have killed me," she said. "I was most emotional about the reason I needed the bilateral mastectomy—I had cancer. It was a devastating, shocking, and overwhelming experience."

Robin has learned a great deal from her experience; she's beyond thankful that things turned out as well as they did, all conditions considered. "Cancer and losing my breasts taught me so much, but most important how to find gratitude," she said. "I'm grateful to have been diagnosed with early-stage breast cancer. My story would have a different ending had I discovered the lump only weeks later or procrastinated on having it examined. I'm grateful to have been forty-three when diagnosed—already having had my desired family of four. I'm also grateful for every doctor and nurse, especially mine, who has dedicated their lives to managing breast cancer. I'm grateful for the countless organizations that raise money to fund research and the women who battled this disease before me. I'm grateful for my new perspective on life."

Robin also had a tremendous support system that made all the difference. "The outpouring of love and kindness has forever changed me," she said. "The positive influence and encouragement of my friends and community were overwhelming. The endless compassion and those connections gave me enormous strength. With so many people rooting for me, there was no way I wouldn't beat cancer."

Robin jokes that she's less prudish now. "Breasts, nipples, sex are all common topics of conversation for me. I have no problem showing people my breasts, because they don't feel like mine—rather, they're a piece of art my plastic surgeon crafted, or even a science project."

I'm especially proud of how empowered Robin feels by an

experience that easily could have floored her. "Even though I lost symbols of my female sexuality, my breasts, hair, and ovaries, I feel more confident and empowered than before cancer," she said. "Although I wish I would have met them under different circumstances, I have come across the smartest, most compassionate and strong women—some of whom I owe my life to because of their medical expertise and others I owe my sanity to because they offered camaraderie during treatment."

Robin has more than come to peace with her new body; she's in awe of its strength. "I'm so ecstatic that my body was successfully able to fight my cancer and heal from my mastectomy," she said. "I love seeing and feeling the strength of my body, given all that I have gone through."

Good Mourning

It's time to take baby steps toward overcoming your greatest worry that's related to the body part you've lost. If you're self-conscious about a leg prosthesis, start by wearing pants, moving to capris, then shorts, then a skirt. Or if your sticking point is talking about what you've been through, practice sharing what happened to you with a best friend or family member who feels safe. You don't have to spend an entire lunch discussing this, but perhaps just coffee and then move on. Talk about what you're experiencing, little by little, and how you're feeling. The more you discuss what you're going through, the less awkward it is for you and for others. This gives loved ones permission to ask questions from a place of genuine concern and not embarrassment.

20

ON LOSING YOUR IDENTITY

*L*osing a friend, a spouse, a job, your home, your hopes and dreams . . . every single loss in this mother-lovin' book is underscored by the loss of identity. That's how far-reaching and potentially painful it is. Because when you lose your identity, Spirit says that you lose a part of your soul. You lose who you are. And there is no greater loss than that. When you lose touch with yourself, you can also experience additional losses like losing a connection to your community and to loved ones. This brings on feelings of sadness, anxiety, and disconnect.

I'm rather secure in who I am, but only because I work hard at it. So many strangers who run into me out and about are often surprised to see that I'm just Theresa from Hicksville, shopping at Target and getting her nails done at the local salon. Regardless of whether I have a television show or travel the world giving readings, I always want to do normal things because I'm a normal person, just like everyone else. I don't let the potential glitz and glam of a being a "celebrity" change who I am. Being authentic is important to me. And when your parents live next door and half the town knows your business, there are plenty of people who keep you straight! I've got a ton of support, which makes being me that much easier.

WHO ARE YOU, REALLY?

Spirit says we have all kinds of identities wrapped up in who we are as people and souls. For instance, you can lose your professional identity, so when you leave a job that gives your days structure and purpose, you might question who you are if not a boss or worker. When you question your faith in a crisis or when someone you love has passed, you can lose a spiritual identity and isolate yourself from God and fellowship at church. If you lose money, you can lose your financial identity—or, if you come into money through a lottery or a big fat inheritance, you might gain a different identity altogether. Changing your financial identity can throw off your sense of security and who you think you are. If you become injured or ill, you might lose your physical identity. You may have been someone who could go regularly to the gym or chase after your grandkids, but now, physical limitations may cause you to not recognize yourself anymore. You can try not to lose your self-worth when you lose your identity, but the two are intertwined.

Spirit says that it's scary when multiple identity losses happen all at once; they can stack up and leave us feeling debilitated. Losing a spouse to a divorce, for instance, can destabilize how you view yourself as a partner, friend, woman, and parent. You might feel an eyelash away from a nervous breakdown or like you're spinning out of control when your identity takes multiple hits. You might try to bandage your wounds and move on, but you need to address them one by one. Spirit says that how you do this is up to you, because we all cope differently.

In an ideal world, you wouldn't allow external factors to rattle who you are. You would allow only your own self-perception to decide who you consider yourself to be. Yet external factors stick to us like raisins to peanut butter on the giant ants-on-a-log that is our identity. You are human, and that means having human interactions and feelings. You must fight hard to ensure that how you view yourself is primarily based on what you feel and not on what others feel about you.

I try hard not to let external factors influence who I am—especially when people are cruel. I put my life out there to make a difference in others' lives, and sometimes that makes strangers feel entitled to insult me and try to mess with my identity. But just because I'm public about a lot of stuff doesn't give anyone the right to mess with it. On social media, people will write, *I hate your nails, I hate your hair*. It's very unfair, and it's cruel. Or they'll ask friends of mine, "Is Theresa as nice as she is on TV?" or "Is she really that dramatic?" Strangers can have a certain perception of who I am, and I have to work hard not to let that toy with how I see myself. I choose every day to have an identity that is valid and real. Nobody can take that away!

CHANGE IS A GOOD THING

When you lose your identity for some reason, realize that it's okay to change and know that being different isn't always bad. Sometimes change is exactly what we need to shake up our self-image and push us outside our comfort zones. Spirit says that life is about change, after all. Nobody is the same person they were last month.

Spirit says that our soul's life goal is to change, grow, and improve from the time that we're born. When life, and your subsequent identity, doesn't turn out the way you think it will, it's easy to worry that the alternative will make you unhappy. But remember, Spirit says that just because you're grieving a past identity doesn't mean that future identities won't someday bring you joy and a renewed sense of purpose. You may no longer be a wife because of a painful divorce, but this may free you up to go back to school, which could then make being a nurse, decorator, or entrepreneur a new part of your identity.

My client Elisa is a great example of this. When she was denied full custody of her daughter after a painful legal battle, she wondered who she could ever be other than a full-time mom. She had spent ten years shaping her own needs, wants, and desires around what her child needed, wanted, and desired. Elisa was a PTA mom, carpool mom, soccer mom, and supermom all rolled into one. But when her divorce settlement took all that away from her, she struggled with knowing what her next step would be.

With more time on her hands than she'd ever had, Elisa decided to throw herself into her work as a writer. She took on professional and passion projects that she wouldn't have had time to accomplish as a full-time mom. Her success grew, and with the money she earned, she was able to treat her and her daughter to fun-filled vacations and memories that she couldn't have afforded previously. What's more, when this mother/daughter duo did spend time together, Elisa was extremely present rather than distracted with the daily juggle that once had occupied her mind. So while Elisa wasn't able to spend as much *quantity* time with her child as she once had, she was able to enrich their *quality* time together, and that made their bond stronger. Elisa realized that she didn't need "full-time mom" to be her identity and that, in fact, wearing fewer hats in her own life, as well as her daughter's, was more fulfilling for both of them.

It's key to remember that your identity will never be what it was before it was lost, and you can't retrace your steps or get in a time machine to go back to that place. Instead, you have to accept that your identity is different now and work on who you believe you are from that point on. A lot of times, it's not your choice to lose your identity. If your child goes to college and leaves you with an empty nest, your identity changes. It's the same with retirement or illness. Related identity changes happen to you, but it's your job to see that they're happening *for* you.

My client Merideth, at the age of thirty-eight, was flying high on a very successful work life in public relations that she had spent years building. In November 2014, however, Merideth's world imploded when she suffered a massive stroke that left her fighting for her life and unable to walk, talk, or speak. It was a terrifying experience. After five years of rehabilitation, she's still not back to the form she was in before the incident. Her recovery journey has been filled with painful milestones and roller-coaster moments.

"Finding a new norm and rebuilding my identity has been a much longer process than I ever expected," said Merideth. "My high-profile job and multitasking parenting skills defined who I was before the stroke. Then my identity changed overnight. I've had to rebuild who I am and understand who this new person is that lives in my body; it's been a humbling, painful, and honest journey." Merideth said that not being able to think as clearly as she once did or physically perform tasks that she once could has taken its toll. "I was a superhero, supermom, superbusinesswoman, yet today I'm a work in progress," she told me.

Merideth realizes that reclaiming her identity means integrating the old with the new. "My husband and I had to rebuild our relationship based on our past and what we wanted in the future," she said. "And my son and I had to rebuild our trust that I wasn't going to die. Even though my clients stuck by me during my recovery, this new post-stroke businesswoman has had to integrate her prior skills with a newer, slower, and more thoughtful pace. I'm grateful that everyone around me is so accepting of how I've mixed the past with the present, because it's been a real learning curve and exercise in acceptance and allowance."

Even so, Merideth said that it's in her nature to always keep "climbing and trying to adjust and create a new normal, as I have no other choice. I can't sit by and not live to the fullest. What's helped has been honesty, patience, and allowing myself to mourn the loss," she said. Merideth has grieved, but she hasn't allowed that grief to stop her from re-creating an identity that she can wholly embrace. The best part about an identity is that you have the chance to define and redefine it, as you wish for it to be. This can be upsetting, or it can be exciting and refreshing; the perspective is up to you.

LOSING CULTURAL IDENTITY

A person who is displaced because they have left one culture for another—whether that's through moving to a new country, state, or even neighborhood—can experience a shift in cultural identity. Familiar smells and traditions are lost. They may not recognize themselves in their new clothes, or they may feel out of place around new foods and accents. They may feel like a stranger in a strange land, because their cultural identity has shifted, and they might not know who they are anymore.

Mantra: I've learned from who I once was and am proud of who I've become.

When you are a transplant, you lose your identity and a sense of who you are becoming. My friend Niklas moved to the United States from Finland in 2012 and has mixed feelings about feeling culturally displaced. There are moments when he feels he's lost his identity, and he misses some of his Finnish habits, like having a sauna. But he still communicates with his Finnish relatives via Skype. "Mostly I miss all my old friends who are in Finland," he said. "Here in the United States, it's difficult for me to get friends, and while people are more social here, it is a shallow socialness. We Finns are maybe more difficult to get close to, but when we make a friendship, it stays forever." Of all the familiar smells, sights, and sounds that he misses most, Niklas said he really misses the atmosphere inside the locker room of his old ice hockey team. "But not the smell!" he laughed. He can feel like a stranger in the US and sometimes lacks a sense of place. "From time to time, I feel that I'm not Finnish anymore, and I'm not American either, so who am I? I'm nobody in particular!"

All that being said, Niklas works hard to integrate his old life with his new one. "I long for my home from time to time, but nowadays, I feel that my home is here, and I'm a visitor only when I'm visiting Finland. I take what I can from my identity there and try to integrate it with my identity here with my family." When he's feeling displaced or a little out of sorts about living here, Niklas says that he likes watching a Finnish movie, listening to Finnish music, and calling Finnish friends to catch up.

Because we have so many identities wrapped up in who we are as one person, Spirit says that the possibility for self-reinvention is endless—in a good way. Be open to these changes, and they will be easier to accept and embrace. Your identity can be what you make of it.

Good Mourning

Create a vision board that's split into three parts: one for who you were, one for who you are now, and one for who you want to be in the future. Cut images from magazines that represent all these parts of you and notice how beautifully you can mix and match them to create the person you want to be.

21

ON LOSING YOUR WILL TO ENDURE

So this topic is a heavy one for me. I've never experienced a loss so tormenting that it has caused me to lose my desire to keep going, but I've channeled enough sorrow to understand the impulse. I personally think there's always a reason to go on if you look hard enough for it—mostly because it's my nature to be optimistic—but I also get how hopelessness and the course of things can cause people to feel like tomorrow just won't be any better.

Everything I know about this topic, I know from channeling Spirit, and they always insist that if you can just push through your pain each day, then time will help heal these wounds. Make it a goal to get out of bed every morning and get yourself to an early bedtime; by simply making it through another day, you'll have something to celebrate. Life can be hard, and when the going gets rough, you must dig deep to find your will to endure.

LOSING IT ALL

A person loses their will to endure when they feel like everything has become too much to handle. Their hopes and dreams feel pointless, they lose faith, they believe they'll never experience joy again—or at least joy that will outweigh the negative impulses they currently feel. I know what you're thinking, and losing your will to endure doesn't have to imply a desire to die, by the way. You might lose your job and then lose your will to go back to school or continue looking for new opportunities. You could lose your home and then lose your determination to rebuild and start over. You could lose trust in your spouse, and then lose your will to work on your relationship and find love again. Losing your will to endure is simply about giving up the pursuit and path you're currently on. It's about feeling so discouraged that you don't want to better yourself and do the work that it takes to try a new avenue that could bring about happiness.

I would never judge someone for losing their will to endure; it is simply a point of exasperation, a feeling that there is nowhere else to go. It's also the only topic in this book where Spirit doesn't tell you to recognize that things could be worse. When you lose your will to endure, you are at rock bottom. Things can't get worse. Spirit has compassion when you're at the end of your rope. They encourage you to gently do what you can to get better, even if that means taking it one hour at a time, until your life slowly turns a corner.

My client Julia understands what it's like to lose her will to go on. For two years, she suffered from neurological Lyme disease and chemical/environmental sensitivities that made her unable to comfortably go out in public and live in her home around her family. So she moved into an apartment as a temporary respite, during which time her husband served her with divorce papers. He told her that he "couldn't deal with any more illness" and that she'd be hearing from his lawyer that week.

Julia was completely blindsided. The couple had a six-year-old child at the time, who hung in the balance. On top of struggling to find doctors who could help Julia heal, she suffered from her husband's rejection and had to fight for shared custody of her child. The pressure and sadness that she felt weighed on her like a boulder.

This cumulative situation brought Julia immense suffering, and some days, it was a challenge for her to even stand upright. "At times, the pain and pressure were too much to bear," Julia confided in me. "On a good day, I'd stay in bed until noon and cry these deep, heaving sobs. On my worst days, I'd ask God to either heal me or if that wasn't His plan, to take my life. I believed that I could do more for my son as a soul in Heaven, loving and guiding him in spirit, than as a human being in a broken body."

Nobody could help Julia see the point of slogging through her daily life, not even for her beautiful son. Her depression was so thick, you could cut it with a knife. Julia couldn't see a way out of her misery and the accumulating losses that came with it— loss of identity, health, marriage, home, familiarity, safety, control, finances, and more. She began to lose hope in God too, though she continued to fervently pray for an answer. Though Julia saw a therapist and had a small army of supportive friends around her, it wasn't enough to bolster her will to endure. It wasn't until her health, with the help of an integrative doctor, showed small signs of improvement that she was able to recapture her will, start working again, and find a reason to get up each morning and embrace the day with her usual gusto. Her will gradually returned, and her energy began to realign with God's purpose for her. Slowly, she began to heal.

LOSING YOURSELF AFTER LOSING A LOVED ONE

Many situations can cause you to lose your will to endure, but losing a loved one—especially a child—is definitely a scenario that I often see. I'll never forget reading a woman whose son had drowned. When I channeled the young man's soul, it said to his mom, "I know that you want to be with me, but it's not your time to die. Your soul can't be with me in that way, but my soul is with you every day, and when it *is* your time, we'll meet again." He also wanted her to know that he had been with her when she'd looked through old photos, and he asked that she remember him as he was in those pictures—smiling, happy, and without a care in the world. He also wanted her to live without blame, shame, or regrets around his passing. I could feel that the mother had lost hope and a sense of purpose when her son died, and she couldn't imagine how she was to go on without him in her life.

A similar scenario came up when I channeled the soul of a woman's daughter who said to her mother, "You have to take care of yourself, and you can't be with me now." The woman had been praying to God that He take her from this world. The woman cried to me, "My daughter was my entire life; she was my everything. I don't know how to live without her." I felt so bad for this heartbroken mother. Typically, when a person feels as lost as this woman did, Spirit will offer a suggestion about how she might find spiritual peace and overcome her suffering—start a foundation in her daughter's honor, join a grief support group at church, or funnel her maternal energy into bonding with her goddaughter or a friend's child. But when someone also loses their will to endure, Spirit holds their proverbial tongues, because a person at this point is too fragile and there is little anyone can say to raise their energy. Spirit simply sends compassion and love.

There's something about the finality of losing a loved one that can push us to the brink. If you lose a job or a friendship, you can always find another. But when a person dies, you can't replace that person or their role in your life. And while losing the will to endure is something a lot of people feel, the severity of it is different for everyone. In all cases, grief and loss take over and eclipse the will to push on.

PUTTING ONE FOOT IN FRONT OF THE OTHER

When you're at this point, Spirit says it may help to pray to Saint Jude, who represents healing to me, and the Blessed Mother, who symbolizes compassion and nurturing. And of course, you should also turn to God and ask for strength to move forward in your life. You can also ask Spirit for validation that you're on the right track and to send you signs that you're surrounded by love and support. Ask that your sorrow be lifted and carried away by a fleet of beautiful angels.

When you're feeling this low, Spirit says to simply let it out as best you can. Crying is a great tool because it's an emotional release and can be cleansing. You can also scream, kick, and punch a pillow if you need to. Do this as often as your heavy feelings come. But after you have a moment, Spirit suggests that you try your best to create a new plan for yourself or do an activity that encourages you to better yourself as a person.

Say you've lost a child in a drunk driving accident and are

grieving that loss so hard that you don't want to leave your bed. Take the time you need to feel sad, think, and reflect. But then recognize that as painful as it is, your life has now changed, and you need to fill your new normal with things that inspire you to get up every morning and start your day. It can feel more motivating to do things for others than to do them for yourself, so come up with a plan to do just one activity that might help another person find peace or understanding related to your heartache—perhaps you can speak at a school about the perils of drunk driving or start a scholarship in your child's name. The goal is to reestablish a purpose or create a series of small goals for yourself so that you can move forward with your life.

THE MORE YOU SUFFER, THE LESS YOU CAN ENDURE

Cumulative pain can also cause us to lose our will to endure over the years. My friend Mary's father had a difficult life, and through a series of heartbreaks, he finally lost his will to live. "If you had told me someone could will themselves to die," Mary said, "I would not have believed you. But then, I watched my dad as he lost his will to endure."

Mary described her father as a kind and quiet man who had seen his share of hardship throughout his life. "He was two years old when his mother died in the flu epidemic of 1918, and he and all of his siblings were packed up and taken to an orphanage in Washington, DC," she said. "His father was in the navy and was told that the orphanage was the best place for the children. He was also advised not to visit, as it would cause the children pain each time he left." Mary's father stayed in the orphanage until he was seventeen years old, when a relative was called to pick him up, sign the paperwork, and enlist him in the Marines.

Mary's dad fought in the Korean War, and on a trip home, he met and married her mother. She was the love of his life. They had five children, and Mary was the youngest, born ten years after the others. When she was just five years old, her mother died from colon cancer. For months after her excruciating death, Mary's dad cried during the day and screamed out in his sleep at night. "I believe it was at that point that even though Dad held it together for the family, his emotional life began to unravel," Mary said. "He met and married the first woman who came along. She was on the hunt for a husband, and even though she didn't want the five children who were involved, she married him anyway."

Mantra: Today might be hard, but I'm determined to have a better future.

It was only after Mary's dad and his new wife said "I do" that it became apparent that this woman, whom Mary called "the Charmer," was a chain-smoking child abuser who would get drunk and attack anyone in her path. Yet no matter how much chaos she caused, Mary's dad stayed in the marriage because (1) good Catholics don't get divorced, and (2) the Charmer had persuaded him that no other woman on earth would want a man with five children. "My dad endured, one step after the other, one day after the other, and one year after the other," Mary said. "Throughout it all, he was kind to me. I was his daughter and his friend." He did all this while shouldering the sadness and burdens of his life.

Mary remembers that her dad once told her that if he ever got sick, he could handle being in a wheelchair, but he would rather die than be in a diaper as an adult. "One day, I got the call that my seventy-six-year-old father had fallen and had some trouble with his speech," Mary said. "It was a brain tumor. He needed to have surgery to have the tumor removed. The good news was that the tumor was benign, and they didn't think he was going to die." The surgery went well, and Mary's dad went home. While he recovered, he had to practice his speech and writing, and sadly, he had to wear a diaper— "the dreaded diaper," as Mary called it—in case of accidents.

Shortly after, Mary's dad began to talk to her about death and dying. "It's my time," he'd say, and Mary would insist, "No, Dad, they said you will recover." He'd remind Mary that all their relatives had died by age seventy-seven and that it was now his time too. With that, Mary would tell him, "No, Dad. That was in the old days when people didn't go to doctors or take care of their health." No matter what she said, Mary's father wouldn't budge on the fact that he was going to pass, and even though she said he didn't have a particularly strong faith, he wasn't at all afraid. In fact, she hadn't seen him so calm, strong, and with such tremendous resolve for many years. "Over and over, despite not having a terminal condition, his will to live was slipping away, and he wanted me to know, 'It's my time,'" Mary said.

When Mary's dad's birthday approached, he asked his daughter what they should do since "this one might be the last." Mary shook her head at his refrain and chose for them to spend time together at his home. She decided to introduce him to the magnificent Three Tenors—Plácido Domingo, José Carreras, and Luciano Pavarotti—on video. Mary's dad loved the gesture, and at the end of the video he said, "This was the best thing ever. Remember this day."

Mary said that if someone were telling her this story, she'd be thinking, *I know where this is going . . . this guy is going to com-*

mit suicide. But Mary's dad didn't take his own life. Days after his birthday, on a beautiful spring afternoon, her father lay down, closed his eyes, took one last peaceful breath, and was gone. It was his time after all.

Spirit says that we are all given a window in which we are destined to pass, and Mary's father had an intuitive knowing that he was within his. He gave up the ghost, so to speak, and surrendered to his heart's desire.

Good Mourning

Create a poster that represents what you'd like your life to look like, with goals that give you something to look forward to achieving now and in the future. This poster can be inspired by a current loss that's bringing you down—perhaps the loss of your financial stability, faith, identity, or good health. Clip images, words, poems, writings—you name it—and glue them to your poster to represent what you want your tomorrow to look and feel like. When you're finished, this collage will represent your vision for your future, and each time you look at it with positivity and optimism, you will help manifest it into reality. It will also act as a reminder to you to actively pursue the goals that you have posted. Don't rely just on God and Spirit to bring these opportunities to you or for the Law of Attraction to invite them; you must pray *and* do, in order to get. Show the universe what you want, then put yourself out there and call in the magic that will bring it to life.

22

ON LOSING CONFIDENCE OVER PAST CHOICES

When we talk about losing confidence over our past choices, we're essentially talking about regret. And when we're thinking about our regrets, it's important that we look at them from the right perspective so that we can heal without feeling any negativity as an aftershock. We have to consider our frame of mind at the time that we made the choice that caused our regret and find a way to be okay with our past decisions. That might mean reframing the choice in our minds, asking for forgiveness, and/or even forgiving ourselves, depending on how the regret tears us up inside.

LESSONS LEARNED

Spirit says that one way to heal from a past regret is to recognize that at the time, the choice or decision that you made served a purpose. The decision might not serve you now or you might feel bad about what you did, but if that's the case, consider it a lesson learned. Use regrets to educate yourself on what matters to you.

Perhaps you punished your son by taking away his technology for a week, but in retrospect, you feel that was a little harsh. Don't beat yourself up over this past choice, because it seemed like a good idea at the time. View it instead as a lesson learned—next time, you'll take away his tech for only a few days.

Here's a silly example: I went out the other night and had a few cocktails and then ate pasta with bread and had dessert—a spectacular meal that I easily could have regretted, but I chose not to. I loved it; it was *delicious*. If I dwelled on my regrets over the calories and carbs I consumed, I'd have ruined my day. Instead, I just ate healthier the next day, exercised, and drank a lot of water. I moved on. I didn't want to stay in a negative headspace, and harping on my regrets would have kept me there. When I saw that I was up three pounds, I replaced feeling regret with learning from my mistake—if I want to keep the pounds down, I can still indulge but maybe cut down on a drink and skip dessert.

Regret relates to things that you wish had been different or better in the past, and those things continue to affect you now. This can cause grief that weighs heavily on your mind and heart if you don't process it and move on in a healthy way. You might regret not spending more time with your children when they were young because you worked so much, or eating too much sugar, which led to health complications. It's natural to feel regret but realize that it's also a dead-end feeling. You can't go back in time to redo your past—you can't relive your relationships with your children or change your previous sugar consumption. What you *can* do is learn from your regret and change your patterns of behavior. You can be more mindful with loved ones and tweak your diet so that you're living your happiest, healthiest, and most regret-free life.

One of the problems with regret is that when you look back,

you go over and over the incident in your mind, and then it has the potential to turn into guilt and shame. We typically cope with past shame, guilt, and regret by stuffing our feelings inside rather than processing them. We can then become resentful, angry, and defensive. This might happen with an argument and how you feel you handled yourself during it.

Guilt, shame, and regret often get lumped together when I channel one of those feelings related to a past choice. Spirit says that it's hard to feel one without experiencing the others. When you grieve a past choice, you also go into what Spirit calls "coulda/woulda/shoulda" land. It serves no purpose to say what you could, would, or should have done differently because, again, you can't go back in time and change the choices and decisions that you made that might have led to a different outcome. Coulda/woulda/shoulda is especially dangerous because you don't know whether your hypothetical redo would have led to a different ending anyway; you're thinking in terms of a fantasy and not reality. So collectively, guilt, shame, regret, and the coulda/woulda/shoulda trio are all related, negative emotions that will eat up your soul and leave you with a degraded sense of self. It's better to promise yourself that you'll never again make a decision like the one you regret and consider it a lesson learned.

FLIP THE COIN

When you're tempted to feel regret, Spirit often says to look at the opposite side of the coin; this tactic works with both heavy incidents that weigh on your heart and daily challenges that matter but aren't life-changing. So if you regret not being in the room when your grandfather passed and not being able to say goodbye, flip the coin and think about the memories you have from when he was alive and you were together. In a more everyday example, if you regret the fact that you couldn't hit the beach when you were on vacation because it rained for three of five days, focus instead on the card games you played and music you listened to while you were bonding with your loved ones inside. You wouldn't have had those experiences and conversations without the downpours. Spirit says there's always a bright side to every cloudy situation.

Regrets can come and go quickly like a storm, or they can hang out in your mind and have long-term consequences that rob you of happiness in the moment and in the long run. Regrets can keep you from making confident choices and decisions in the future, because you might not trust yourself or you worry about hurting others— whatever the fallout is for the scenario you regret. Whether you second-guess yourself with relationships, doctors, future vacations, and so on, you don't want to feel insecure about your choices going forward because you've beaten yourself down for your past.

In related news, this is super interesting: a study found that regrets related to things you *wished* you'd said or done stay with you longer than things you *actually* said or did, which are more powerful in the short term. In other words, wishing you'd been honest with your mom and told her she was mean to you during an argument will stay with you much longer than simply calling her mean in the moment, which will cause bad feelings for only a little while. And if you don't like your daughter's boyfriend, you'll feel worse about not saying how you feel than telling her the truth, even if it doesn't come out the right way and you think twice about it later. Knowing this, you can reduce regrets by simply saying what you feel in the moment—but also being mindful of the words that you use. If you say what you mean, and say it carefully, you won't have anything to regret, and you will be able to move on without an unrelenting burden.

PREEMPT THOSE REGRETS

Because I know from Spirit that regrets can tear a person up, I do my best to get ahead of them so that I don't have any regrets in the future. For instance, it upsets me that I don't spend more time with my parents when I'm on the road for work, and so I find every chance I can to tell them how much I love, appreciate, miss, and treasure them. I want to be sure that they know exactly how I feel about them, because I don't want to look back someday and regret that I wasn't expressive enough about my feelings because I was too busy or distracted. I don't want to wish I'd said something and have that eat me up inside for years to come.

Though we can feel regret when we look back on our actions and believe we should have done something differently, you must realize that you can't change what's in the past. What you can do is try to preempt any negative feelings that might arise in the future, like I do, and allow regretful situations from the past to change you for the better once you've learned from them. It's important to heal your past regrets, or they will lead to additional losses, such as the loss of identity or feelings of safety, and any existing guilt or shame will be compounded by bitterness, hatred, and despair. The more negative feelings you accumulate, the longer it will take you to feel better.

I know a woman named Terri who did a tremendous job of getting ahead of her regrets when she found herself in a dire situation. Terri's husband—an abusive alcoholic who had threatened to kill her, the kids, and himself—abandoned the family on

Christmas morning after their four children had opened their presents. Terri had implored him not to go on that particular day because she felt it would mark their kids forever. At the time, the children were ages four, seven, thirteen, and sixteen.

Mantra: I have regret and disappointment, but I will let go and forgive—for myself.

Nonetheless, Terri's husband left her family on Christmas, in a terrible situation from which it was hard to recover. In addition to the emotional toll of their broken relationship, he left her with nothing financially. "My ex told me he would bring me to poverty when I filed for divorce, and he did," she said. Terri went from living in one of the nation's wealthiest towns with a large home, pool, gardener, nannies, you name it, to living on welfare and feeding her children from food pantries. She was forced to rent homes without heat, never owning enough blankets and barely having the money to feed her kids fruits and vegetables. At one point, Terri sold her engagement ring for just $80, all so she could feed her family for a week. "We had a picnic on the floor that night," she said. "It felt extravagant." To get by, Terri would repeat, "I'd rather live in an attic room with a crust of bread than feast in a castle with no peace." She repeatedly played the song "All You Need Is Love" for the kids, as they danced around the house, hoping to normalize a traumatic situation.

In order to survive, Terri had to strategize how to manage her children's grief and mitigate any further damage for their sake and her own, so that she and the children wouldn't have overwhelming regrets. As you can imagine, all four kids had grief issues from the sudden loss of their home, father, finances, and mother's attention, as she worked four jobs to pay the rent and put food on the table. They often felt as if they'd lost both their parents.

Terri did her best to manage her children's needs but had to prioritize. "I had to decide which child to heal first and whose grief would take them down the hardest," she said. "It felt like a 'Sophie's choice.'" When Terri's husband left, her oldest daughter, the sixteen-year-old, had just given birth. Three months later, Terri gave her her blessing to live with her soon-to-be in-laws. Around the same time, Terri's son was in intense counseling five days a week. Terri struggled with juggling her schedule and managing his intense anger. She felt she needed to use tough love, as he was headed for addiction, which had been normalized in the family. Terri wanted to get ahead of this. With her eldest daughter cared for, Terri put all her effort into getting her son into a treatment program for ten months. "It was so painful to see him head down a route of addiction," she said. "I had to stabilize him." Terri then sent her two remaining daughters to her mom's house in New Jersey for two years while she got back on her feet. "I was exhausted, broke, depressed, and had to deal with broken kids," she said. "Keeping them all with me would have created more grief, because I couldn't provide a stable environment right away." She feared that her kids' grief would follow them through life if it wasn't dealt with properly.

While her kids were away, Terri saw a therapist and grieved the fantasy of what she had wanted her marriage to be versus the reality of how it had played out. She did self-care, spiritual work, and volunteered at an AIDS hospice, which kept her grounded and helped her recognize that suffering is part of human life. "I did what I could to remind myself that life is tough, and we're all in this together. I felt so alone. My battle fatigue was huge," she said. Terri kept her focus on creating love, vision, and hope for her family after their intense bout with poverty and pain.

All along, Terri said that she felt guided "by a higher force that I had to trust. I had to believe that I had nothing to lose." She felt intuitively reassured that she was making the best choices she could for her family, especially to avoid feeling future shame, blame, and regret. Terri said she leaned on God a lot and learned to accept what was happening to her and that conditions in life could change on a dime. "I needed to feel like I was doing my best, so I told God to take this burden from me because I couldn't do my best without Him. I put a lot of faith in blind trust," she said. "I relied fully on Spirit, and God's timing, and I had to trust and surrender like no other time in my life."

Terri pushed through her pain and persevered. After such profound loss, the only thing she had to hold on to was hope. "I knew it was a doorway to wellness eventually," she said. "Gratitude—that my family remained intact, that divorcing my husband was the right choice, that I could support the kids and myself again—kept me fed. Gratitude and patience. We felt the presence of an undeniable love that was supernatural."

It took years, even decades for some issues, before life settled down for the family and they felt like a cohesive unit again. Today, however, Terri is happy and healthy, and her kids lead successful lives and reach out to other people when they are in need. What's more, they understand the value and beauty of miracles, thankfulness, faith, and perseverance. "For us, grief was an enormous teacher," Terri said. The family talks openly about their trials and feels those trials helped them all to grow into the people they are today.

FORGIVING OTHERS AND YOURSELF

When you feel regret, it's important to forgive others for what they may have done to cause this emotion in you and also to forgive yourself, for how you may have reacted or responded to them. The sticky part here is that a person may never apologize for what they've done, yet it still helps you to forgive them so that you can feel relief. Forgiveness is really about your healing, first and foremost.

The thing about forgiveness is that it's simply the release of anger that's bottled up inside you; it doesn't necessarily mean reconciliation or redoing the past. Psychologists say forgiving someone can help elevate your mood, guard against stress, lower anxiety, and decrease depression. Even if the person who hurts you offers an insincere apology or nothing at all, and you regret having engaged with that person in the first place, forgiving yourself is key. Just ignoring or trying to cope with the problem rarely works. Spirit says you must decide to forgive and try to have compassion for the person who hurt you. Think about whether the act was done intentionally or in a difficult circumstance. Try to let go of your upsetting emotions and think about how you may have grown from the experience.

Forgiveness is about being good to others even when they might not have earned your generous behavior. It's something you give to another person because you know it's the right thing to do. Empathy is a big part of forgiveness. Spirit says it might help you to forgive someone who harmed you if you can develop empathy for that person and consider what their own demons might be that led to the event. It also helps to find meaning in your suffering; otherwise, it will lead to a sense of hopelessness, regret, and sadness. Figure out how your suffering has changed you in a positive way. Use this to be a better person.

Bottom line, don't wait for an apology to forgive someone for an incident or situation that you regret being part of. When craving forgiveness from another person, realize that you aren't responsible for other people's actions or words, so you can't expect them to give you an apology because they might not regret their choice or regret it in a way you wish they would. You can't get something from someone that they aren't capable of giving. If someone killed your child in a car accident, you might never get an apology if that person doesn't have the conscience to give you one. If you wish your relationship had gone differently before your marriage ended, your partner may never feel sorry for the ways she contributed to the split and give you the apologies you need to hear. At these times, it is enough for *you* to apologize to or accept apologies from, in both your heart and your imagination, the person and situation causing regrets. You don't need to do this in person. It might help to write a letter from the other person to yourself that says everything you need to hear to heal from the regret and move on. I once read a quotation that really hit home: "I never knew how strong I was until I had to forgive someone who wasn't sorry and accept an apology that I never received." *Bam!* How true and powerful is that?

When it comes to forgiving yourself, the goal is to get rid of the internal guilt and shame that you might feel for what you've done. Honor that you aren't perfect, and that you're human, after all; also, if you've gone against your standards, don't slip into self-loathing. Take good care of yourself during this time; move toward self-compassion. A sincere apology, free of conditions and expectations, will go a long way toward receiving forgiveness in your own heart and soul. You can do this while looking at yourself in the mirror, or during a meditation.

And if you've hurt someone else, and you regret that, start by admitting that you were at fault and take accountability for the hurt you caused. Then find the lessons that you've learned and figure out how to avoid hurting people in the same way in the future. You may want to apologize to the person whom you hurt and try to improve their life in some way to minimize your regrets. Reach out with a card or send them a sincere text. Be genuine and show that you care. Find another opportunity to say and demonstrate what you feel. You can't change what you said or did to make a person feel bad, but you can find a chance to apologize or improve the situation.

Every new day is an opportunity to either grow our souls or abandon our desire to be better versions of ourselves. Which route will you choose? Daily losses come and go, and it's up to you to work through them and feel happier for it. Making the most of Spirit's tools will help you be the best person you can and get through the daily trials we face on this planet. Everyday losses don't need to take you down when you use them as opportunities to become stronger, wiser, and more capable of spreading compassion, goodness, and love to yourself and the world around you.

Good Mourning

Think of a regret that you have, perhaps over an argument you had with a loved one or a comment you made that you wish you hadn't. Perhaps you didn't acknowledge someone in a way that you should have. Take the time now to send them a genuine note to see how they're doing. Apologize if it's appropriate, or simply send a sincere hello to see how they feel. Rather than ignore the incident and pretend it didn't happen, say something to help yourself and the other person move through that regret. Even if your gesture falls on deaf ears, it will help you to heal and move on.

ACKNOWLEDGMENTS

I'd like to thank everyone who helped bring this project to fruition—from friends, family, and colleagues on earth to God and Spirit in Heaven. It takes a multidimensional village to launch a book!

To Kristina Grish, my faithful coauthor and friend. Thank you for all your hard work, as always. You and I both know what it is to experience crummy losses; here's to a fulfilling future ahead!

To Judith Curr, Hilary Swanson, and the entire team at HarperOne who helped usher this book into the world. Thank you for having faith in my idea and vision for it. I also appreciate how you've believed in both me and my gift throughout this project. Cheers to another bestseller!

To Courtney Mullin and Victoria Woods. During my hardest years, you were the most supportive and encouraging duo I ever could have known; thank you for always rooting me on and reminding me to be my best for myself, Spirit, and those I love. Thanks, too, for insisting that I always put my fear aside for the greater good. I wouldn't be where I am without you. You've protected me and my gift, and if anyone wants to know how this all started, I blame you!

To Magilla Entertainment and TLC for not wanting to change me and my gift, and for being willing to throw out the rulebook on production so that I can share my abilities with so many viewers. Thanks, too, to my crew, who's been with me since day one. I am so grateful to you all.

To Rich Super and Mike Mills at Mills Entertainment for putting me and my fancy shoes on a live stage so that everyone can experience Spirit communication, up close and personal. And to Jeff Cohen, my lawyer extraordinaire: I got ninety-nine problems, but my attorney ain't one!

To all my friends, especially Kevin Fuchs, Darrin O'Neil, and Jimmy Oliver, who've known me since I was fourteen years old. Thanks for always having my back and reinforcing how "real" I am to strangers. You guys know the truth!

To everyone in my family, thank you for your support over the years and sorry that so many people badger you for a reading! Thanks to my parents especially, who continue to love and support me in all that I do. I couldn't be who, or where, I am without you. And to my loved ones in Heaven, for guiding, loving, and protecting me as I bring much-needed peace to those in need.

To my brother Michael, for becoming my new, "better half." You've been by my side through it all, especially when I've needed you most these past few years. I'm so lucky to have you.

To Larry and Victoria, for your encouragement and understanding as we navigate our new family dynamic. I love our Trio of Togetherness and how you always stand by me. I know we can get through anything, and I will always support your life choices, just as you support mine.

Last but never least, I am deeply thankful to God and Spirit for giving me my gift and helping me channel in creative ways that bring healing to so many. To the fans and clients who inspire and touch me every day with their optimism, strength, and mind-blowing stories: it's not easy to live in your skin, yet you are able to gracefully persevere. I am so thankful for you all.